MARYLANDERS AT GETTYSBURG

Daniel Carroll Toomey

Toomey Press
Baltimore, Maryland

Toomey Press

P.O. Box 122
Linthicum, MD 21090
410-766-1211

Other books by
Daniel Carroll Toomey

The Civil War in Maryland

A History of Relay, Maryland and the Thomas Viaduct

Index to the Roster of Maryland Volunteers

The Patapsco Guards Independent Company of Maryland Volunteer
Infantry

Baltimore During the Civil War

Book Design and Composition: Cynthia Edmiston, Merrifield Graphics &
Publishing Service, Inc., Baltimore, Maryland
Cover Design: Cynthia Edmiston
Printing: H.G. Roebuck & Son, Inc., Baltimore, Maryland

First Edition 1994
Second Edition 1998

ISBN 0-9612670-3-8

This book is dedicated to each and every
one of you who donated your time, money,
and professional services to help make the
Maryland Memorial at Gettysburg an
outstanding example of why we are proud
to be from the Old Line State.

Contents

Chapter 1: **THE BATTLE** 1

    July 1, 1863 3

    July 2, 1863 7

    July 3, 1863 22

Chapter 2: **THE AFTERMATH** 41

Chapter 3: **THE VETERANS** 49

    The Maryland Confederate Monument 49

        Description of the Maryland Confederate Monument 51

    The Union Monuments 54

        Description of the Monuments 58

    The 50th Anniversary Reunion 73

    The 75th Anniversary Reunion 75

Chapter 4: **THE FINAL TRIBUTE** 79

    The Dedication 80

        Description of the Maryland Memorial 81

Notes 83

Appendix A: List of Casualties in the First Maryland Infantry Bat. 87

Appendix B: Official List of Casualties (Union) 91

Appendix C: Roster of Maryland Soldiers in National Cemetery 95

Appendix D: Marylanders Attending 75th Reunion in 1938 96

Appendix E: Citizens for a Maryland Monument in Gettysburg 97

Index 98

Introduction

When General Robert E. Lee crossed the Potomac River in June of 1863, he brought with him an army of 75,000 men, 270 pieces of artillery, and the South's best chance to win the war which had now entered its third bloody year. As divisions of Rebel troops moved about southern Pennsylvania at will, General George Gordon Meade was informed in the early hours of June 28 that he had been appointed the new commander of the Army of the Potomac.

Lee planned to live off the rich northern farm land for as long as possible and deliver a crushing defeat to the Union Army in its own back yard. Meade planned to concentrate his army of 85,000 men in a defensive position along Pipe Creek in Carroll County, Maryland, where he would be able to shield both Baltimore City and Washington, D.C. from a Confederate attack. Uncontrolled circumstances brought these two generals and their armies together in one of the most decisive battles in American history—Gettysburg.

Immediately after the battle, citizens of Pennsylvania began efforts which eventually led to the creation of the Gettysburg National Military Park. Today, Gettysburg is the single most recognized Civil War battle in the world and one of the most popular themes in Civil War literature. With this in mind, it is not surprising that the veterans, their descendants, and the states from which they served were proud to be associated with this epic battle.

Maryland's participation in the battle is significant not for the number of men engaged, but for its stunning representation of the Civil War in miniature. When the war began, a large number of Maryland men crossed the Potomac River and enlisted in the Confederate Army. Some formed batteries and regiments under the flag of their native state. Others joined family and friends in state units throughout the Confederacy. At the same time an even greater number of men enlisted in the Union Army. Most, but not all, of these served in Maryland-designated commands.

As the two opposing forces converged on the town of Gettysburg, virtually all the Maryland state units in both armies found themselves on or in supporting positions surrounding Culp's Hill. Only Wesley Culp would bring home the tragedy of our civil war in a sadder fashion when he died on his family's farm as a member of the Stonewall Brigade. Here then is a story of Gettysburg yet to be told—Marylanders at Gettysburg. It is not my intention to identify every citizen of Maryland who participated in the battle. I have instead chronicled the actions of all state units, groups of Marylanders serving in other commands, principal officers, and a representation of individual soldiers serving in both armies.

Daniel Carroll Toomey
Linthicum, Maryland
November, 1994

Acknowledgments

The support group for this book was small, but extremely helpful in the preparation of this work, and shared the author's enthusiasm for the project. First, I would like to thank Erick F. Davis for coming out of retirement to read the manuscript and add significantly to the finished product. I would also like to thank two friends for giving me complete access to their wonderful collections of Maryland images: Gil Barrett for filling the gap with Marylanders in blue and Dave Mark for supplying nearly all the Confederate images used in the book. Finally, I would like to thank Mr. James A. Holechek, Chairman of the Citizens for a Maryland Monument at Gettysburg, for a constant flow of information on the monument and for allowing me to be a part of the project.

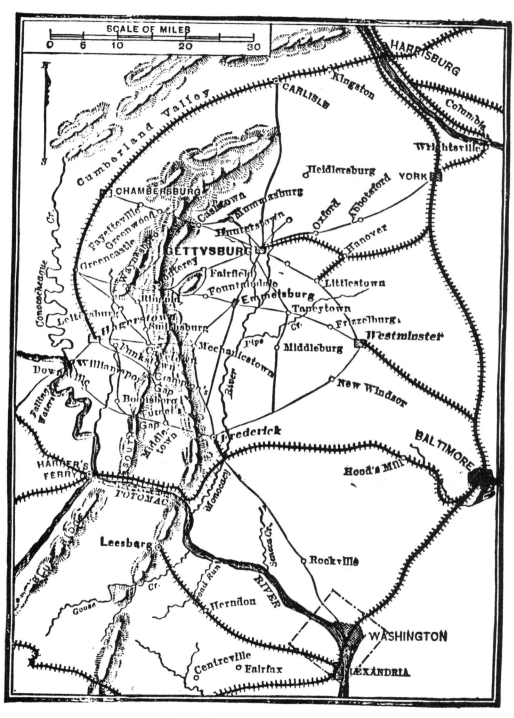

Area of the Gettysburg Campaign.

Lt. Gen. Richard S. Ewell. CSA.

Maj. Gen. Edward Johnson. CSA.

Brig. Gen. George Hume
"Maryland" Steuart. CSA.

Lt. Col. Richard Snowden Andrews.
CSA.

Chapter 1

THE BATTLE

Following the death of General T. J. "Stonewall" Jackson after the battle of Chancellorsville in May of 1863, General Lee was forced to reorganize the Army of Northern Virginia from two corps to three. James Longstreet would command the First Corps. Richard S. Ewell, a veteran of Jackson's many successes in the Shenandoah Valley, assumed command of the Second Corps. A. P. Hill, whose famous Light Division had saved the day at Antietam, was given the Third Corps.

Within the Second Corps could be found many of Jackson's old commands and the greatest concentration of Marylanders in the Army of Northern Virginia. Major General Edward Johnson's Division contained the famous Stonewall Brigade that was once commanded by Maryland born General Charles Winder and had a long association with Maryland troops. Johnson's Assistant Adjutant General was Henry Kyd Douglas—a Marylander who had served on Jackson's staff. Also in the division was the brigade commanded by Brigadier General George Hume "Maryland" Steuart. Steuart's Brigade consisted of three regiments from Virginia, two from North Carolina, and the First Maryland Infantry Battalion. Serving on his staff was First Lieutenant Randolph McKim, an original member of the First Maryland Infantry in 1861. Finally, the divisional artillery was commanded by Lieutenant Colonel Richard Snowden Andrews of Baltimore, Maryland. Andrews' father, Colonel Timothy Patrick Andrews, was Pay Master General of the United States Army at this time. Andrews' Battalion contained two Maryland and two Virginia batteries. (1)

One unit that was temporarily attached to the Second Corps during the campaign was the 35th Battalion of Virginia Cavalry, commanded by Lieutenant Colonel Elijah V. White. White was born near Poolsville in Montgomery County. In 1857, he moved across the Potomac River and bought a farm in Loundon County, Virginia. When the war began he organized a company of cavalry in Leesburg and was elected Captain. (2)

Dave Mark

Lt. Col. Elijah V. White.
35th VA Battalion. CSA.

On October 28, 1862, White's Battalion was mustered into Confederate service by Colonel Bradley T. Johnson, who was then serving on the staff of General J.E.B. Stuart. (3) The battalion, known as The Comanches, was made up of men from both sides of the Potomac.

The Comanches crossed the Potomac River at Shepherdstown and reported to General Ewell at Green castle on June 25. The next day White was ordered to take his battalion of about 250 men and accompany General Jubal A. Early's division to Wrightsville in the hopes of capturing a railroad bridge over the Susquehanna River. Their line of march took them through the quiet town of Gettysburg where a regiment of Pennsylvania militia and a detachment of cavalry had arrived the night before. On the approach of the feared Rebel army, the militia men took off in the direction of Harrisburg. A few were captured, but no injuries were reported on either side, save one overweight militia captain who was accidentally run over by a horse from Company E. The Confederates stayed in town for about 24 hours gathering supplies and horses and then moved on toward York. Thus, White's Battalion was the first group of Marylanders to enter Gettysburg. They would be back in less than a week, but the loss of life for both armies would be much higher. (4)

When the gray legions of the Army of Northern Virginia began crossing the Potomac River in June of 1863, the tranquil lives of many home guard units in Maryland were quickly disrupted. The first of those affected was Company A, Purnell Legion Cavalry. The Purnell Legion was organized at Pikesville in the latter part of 1861. Named for the Postmaster of Baltimore City, William H. Purnell, it consisted of one regiment of infantry, two batteries of artillery, and three companies of cavalry. After a short term of service on the Eastern Shore of Maryland, the legion concept was abandoned and the infantry and artillery transferred to the Army of the Potomac. The three companies of cavalry remained in the state and served as independent commands. (5)

On June 28, Captain Robert E. Duvall was ordered to escort two guns of Rank's Pennsylvania battery from their position on the Monocacy River near Frederick to Baltimore City. En route the tiny convoy almost collided with J.E.B. Stuart's cavalry division at Cooksville. Stuart and his famous captured wagon train were moving across Howard County toward Westminster. Duvall, with 74 men and 2 guns, would have been no match for such a force. He fell back toward the city of Frederick and was fortunate enough to find Colonel John B. McIntosh's First Brigade of the Second Cavalry Division. Both Rank's gunners and the troopers of Company A found themselves part of Pleasonton's Cavalry Corps until the end of the campaign. (6)

JULY 1, 1863

On the night of June 28 Lee learned from James Harrison, an actor from Baltimore and spy for General Longstreet, that a good portion of the Army of the Potomac was as close as Frederick, Maryland, and that Hooker had been replaced by Meade. Both army commanders, Lee and Meade, issued similar instructions to their Corps Commanders—concentrate their divisions, but bring on no general engagement until a clear plan of action could be developed. (7)

On the last day of June General John Buford's cavalry division entered Gettysburg. His mission was not to hold the town but to find the enemy. Local citizens informed him of the comings and goings of Confederate infantry. Buford determined to hold the town the next day and see what would develop. July 1 brought the division of Henry Heth marching down the Chambersburg Pike from Cashtown bent on capturing the shoe factory in Gettysburg. What should have been a minor skirmish between foraging infantry and some cavalry pickets soon brought on the general engagement that both army commanders had sought to avoid. Forced to respond to the Federal build up, General Lee ordered his army to move toward Gettysburg.

As the morning battle developed, Heth pushed two brigades along the pike toward McPherson's Ridge. Davis's Brigade was on the left. The brigade on the right consisted of two Alabama and three Tennessee regiments. It was commanded by one of three Marylanders present during the battle who held the rank of general in the Confederate Army.

Brig. Gen. James Jay Archer.
CSA.

Brigadier General James Jay Archer was born in Bel Air, Harford County in 1817. He served in the Regular Army with the rank of captain and won a brevet to major at Chapultepec during the Mexican War. He resigned his commission in 1861 to become colonel of the Fifth Texas Infantry. Promoted to brigadier general in 1862, Archer fought in every major battle involving the Army of Northern Virginia from Seven Days to Gettysburg. (8)

Waiting on the Confederate advance were the two brigades of Buford's cavalry strung out along Willoughby Run. This thin line of dismounted troopers held up Heth's advance for an hour before they were forced back by infantry moving on their flanks. Thinking he had unsupported Union cavalry on the run, Archer led his brigade across the stream and into McPherson's Woods where he was struck in the flank by the unexpected arrival of the Iron Brigade from the First Corps. Archer and a great number of his men were captured and the rest of the brigade routed. Archer had the dubious honor of being the first general officer captured in the army since Lee had taken command. Imprisoned at Johnson's Island for a year, he returned to the Army of Northern Virginia in poor health and died on October 24, 1864. (9)

In the absence of J.E.B. Stuart's main force, White's Battalion provided an effective cavalry screen when General Early put his division in motion toward Gettysburg on July 1. The Comanches captured some Yankee skirmishers along Rock Creek and sent them to General Gordon's headquarters. (10)

The fighting throughout the afternoon of July 1 was a race to see which army could put more men on the field. Heth renewed his attack with the help of Rodes' Division. On the Union side the hard pressed cavalry and First Corps were greatly aided by the arrival of the Eleventh Corps until Early's Division, moving down the Harrisburg Road, struck the Union right flank. This caused the Union line to break and the survivors fled through the streets of Gettysburg to the sanctuary of Culp's Hill and Cemetery Hill. By 5:00 p.m. Confederate forces controlled the area north and west of Gettysburg and the town itself. At this juncture Lee ordered Ewell to take Cemetery Hill if possible. This would prevent the Federal Army from establishing a new line of defense in the immediate area. Ewell decided to wait for Johnson's men to arrive and start over in the morning with three rested divisions. This gave the Union forces on the two hills the whole night of July 1 to fortify their lines, position guns, and bring up more men. It also gave newly arriving divisions a foundation on which to extend the

Major Ridgely Brown.
1st MD Cavalry. CSA.

Union line along Cemetery Ridge all the way to Little Round Top, thus forming the now famous "Fish Hook" with Culp's Hill being the point of the hook. (11)

The first official Maryland Confederate unit to arrive on the battlefield was the First Maryland Cavalry, temporarily under the command of Major Harry Gilmor. The First Maryland began its existence as Company K, First Virginia Regiment. After one year of service, 18 men formed Company A of the First Maryland in Richmond on May 15, 1862. Ridgely Brown was elected captain. At Winchester the following November, the battalion was formed and Brown was promoted to major. (12)

When the Gettysburg Campaign began, Company A, commanded by Captain Frank Bond, was attached to General Ewell's headquarters to act as guides during the advance through Maryland and Pennsylvania. The balance of the battalion was assigned to Steuart's Brigade at Hagerstown. The First Maryland spent two days in McConnellsburg gathering horses and cattle before reporting to General Ewell on the opening day of the battle. Ewell ordered Gilmor to support the batteries of Page and Carter. Gilmor wisely posted his 200 men in a ravine near the guns to protect them from counter-battery fire. Captain Bond was stationed in Gettysburg with Company A, as Acting Provost Marshal.

Captain Frank Bond.
1st MD Cavalry. CSA.

The next day Major Brown arrived and assumed command of the battalion. He had been recovering from a wound received at Greenland Gap and missed the start of the campaign. During the next two days his companies were detailed on separate assignments and did not take part in the cavalry battle on July 3. During the retreat to the Potomac River, the First Maryland covered the rear of Ewell's wagon train. At Hagerstown Captain Bond was wounded and had to be left behind. He was captured and sent to Point Lookout prison until exchanged in 1864. After the war, he joined the Maryland National Guard and rose to the rank of major general. Frank Bond was one of two Maryland Confederates at Gettysburg to command the Maryland National Guard after the war. (13)

General Johnson was leading his division through Fayetteville when the sounds of the battle reached him. He immediately sent one of his staff officers, Major Henry Kyd Douglas, to report to General Ewell at Gettysburg and inform him that the division was force marching to the scene of conflict and would be ready for a fight when it got there. Having served with both Ewell and Jackson since the beginning of the war, Douglas expected immediate action. He was dumb struck at Ewell's response: "General Lee told me to come to Gettysburg and go no further . . . ." With these words the outcome of the battle was decided before the Lee-Longstreet controversy could even begin, for Culp's Hill was to the Union right flank what Little Round Top was to its left. Sandy Pendleton, also a former aide to Jackson and Ewell's Chief of Staff, lamented: "Oh, for the presence and inspiration of Old Jack for just one hour!" (14)

Steuart's Brigade arrived at Gettysburg a little before dusk July 1 and was ordered to go into camp on the southeast side of the town. It consisted of the following units and commanders:

1st Maryland Battalion—Lt. Col. J. R. Herbert
1st North Carolina Regiment—Lt. Col. H. A. Brown
3rd North Carolina Regiment—Maj. W. M. Parsley

10th Virginia Regiment—Col. E. T. H. Warren
23rd Virginia Regiment—Lt. Col. S. T. Walton
37th Virginia Regiment—Maj. H. C. Wood (15)

Before continuing our narrative, some explanation is required as to the true identity of the First Maryland Battalion. When the war began in 1861, Maryland seemed a likely candidate for secession. However, in May of that year Federal troops occupied Annapolis and Baltimore City dashing the hopes of secessionists in the state. Many young men believed this to be a second American Revolution and made their way across the Potomac River to form companies in Richmond and Harpers Ferry. The First Maryland Infantry Regiment was organized at Harpers Ferry on June 16, 1861. Its staff officers were Colonel Arnold Elzey, Lt. Colonel George H. Steuart, and Major Bradley T. Johnson. All three of these men rose to the rank of general in the Confederate Army before the end of the war. (16)

The First Maryland Regiment served in Ewell's Division of Jackson's Corps during the first half of 1862. It was periodically attached to the Stonewall Brigade commanded at the time by fellow Marylander General Charles Winder. On August 17, 1862, the regiment was mustered out of the Confederate Army as its term of enlistment was determined to be for one year only. (17) At this point in the war there still remained a small reservoir of manpower in the Old Line State that was eager to join the Confederacy. A number of officers and enlisted men from the old First went to Richmond to organize these recruits into a new regiment. Failing to secure enough men to form a full regiment, the First Maryland Battalion was mustered into Confederate service in October of 1862. It was commanded by Lt. Colonel James R. Herbert and Major William W. Goldsborough. It was not until 1864 that the battalion assumed the identity of the Second Maryland. However, in post-war writings it is almost exclusively referred to as the Second Battalion from its inception. (18)

JULY 2, 1863

On the morning of July 2, the Stonewall Brigade found itself on the extreme left of the Confederate line. With J. E. B. Stuart's cavalry still unaccounted for, it was forced to "play cavalry" and screen the army's flank. Moving across Brinkerhoff's Ridge, the brigade skirmished with the Ninth Massachusetts Infantry, which was soon relieved by real cavalry from General David Gregg's Second Division. (19)

The Union cavalry had been marching nonstop since its chance meeting with the Purnell Legion and arrived at Gettysburg at 11 a.m. on the second day of the battle. After a few hours rest, Gregg was ordered to relieve the infantry. He ordered McIntosh's brigade to move down the Hanover Road and take on the Rebel infantry. The brigade consisted of five regiments including the First Maryland and the recently acquired Company A of the Purnell Legion with the guns of Captain William D. Rank's battery. The two pieces of artillery were planted in the road and began to shell the Rebels on Brinkerhoff's Ridge. Around 6 p.m., the Third Pennsylvania Regiment advanced to the right of the Hanover Road with two companies dismounted as skirmishers. The skirmish line was soon extended to the left by the arrival of the Purnell Legion company and two squadrons of the First New Jersey.

A well-built stone wall ran across the top of the ridge. Both sides immediately perceived the importance of its shelter and charged for the wall. Fire from Rank's guns slowed the pace of the Second Virginia enough to allow the Union cavalrymen to reach their objective first and deliver a withering volley of carbine fire at the range of only twenty feet. The Confederates then fell back about 200 yards to a sheltered position and continued to exchange fire with the Union cavalry until after sundown. At 10 p.m., McIntosh's brigade was withdrawn from the line and ordered to camp for the night near the Reserve Artillery Train on the Baltimore Pike. (20)

Marylanders in blue began to arrive on the battlefield in earnest on July 2. The First Regiment Potomac Home Brigade reported with Lockwood's Brigade about 9 a.m. It was the largest Maryland unit in either army, numbering 739 officers and enlisted men. The regiment was originally recruited to be part of a brigade consisting of four infantry regiments and four companies of cavalry. Its area of operation was to be in the western part of the

Brig. Gen. Henry H. Lockwood.
USA.

state and along the Potomac River. Only three regiments were organized by the spring of 1862 and the brigade concept was discontinued. The First Potomac Home Brigade saw very little action during the first two years of the war and spent most of its time guarding the Baltimore and Ohio Railroad. During the Antietam Campaign it was part of the garrison captured at Harpers Ferry. After being exchanged, it was assigned to duty in Southern Maryland as part of Lockwood's Brigade. (21)

With a major Confederate invasion at hand, the Federal Government issued a wholesale call up of home guard troops. On June 25, Brigadier General Henry H. Lockwood was ordered to march immediately with the One Hundred and Fiftieth New York and the First Potomac Home Brigade to Monocacy Bridge where he was to join the Army of the Potomac. The First Eastern Shore Infantry was added to the list the next day. (22) During the battle, Lockwood's Brigade became part of General Alpheus S. Williams' First Division of the Twelfth Army Corps. (23)

Immediately upon its arrival, the First Potomac Home Brigade was put on the extreme right of the line on Culp's Hill and began to throw up earthworks. This was about 9 a.m. The regiment saw no action until 5 p.m. when it and the New Yorkers were pulled out of the line and ordered to the Union left flank where Longstreet's Corps was attacking. As General Smith and his staff crossed Cemetery Ridge they met Lt. Colonel Freeman McGilver, who told them that his artillery brigade was without infantry support and some of his guns were already lost. Williams ordered Lockwood's small brigade to retake the guns and plug the hole in the Union line. Colonel William P. Maulsby ordered the First Potomac Home Brigade to fix bayonets and led them in a charge across the Trostle Farm that recaptured three Napoleons belonging to Bigelow's Battery and chased the Twenty-First Mississippi all the way back to the Peach Orchard.

The New York regiment followed immediately behind the Marylanders and pulled the recaptured guns to safety by hand. Both regiments were exposed to artillery fire that injured 30 men in the First Potomac Home Brigade, which Colonel Maulsby said were not counted in the final report for the regiment. The Marylanders stayed in a ravine near the Peach Orchard for several hours after the charge. The adjutant and surgeon used this time to gather up wounded from the day's fighting. Assistant Surgeon James Willard remained on the field most of the night until ambulances could be found to remove them to safety. After sundown, Lockwood's Brigade was ordered to return to its original position on Culp's Hill. (24)

Other Marylanders arrived with the Twelfth Army Corps as well. The Third Maryland Infantry, commanded by Colonel Joseph M.

Col. Joseph M. Sudsburg.
3rd MD Infantry. USA.

Sudsburg, represented one of the best combat regiments from the state. It had fought in the Shenandoah Valley, Cedar Mountain, Antietam, and Chancellorsville. (25) The number of men present for duty on July 2 bore testimony to the hard campaigning of the regiment. A new regiment was mustered into service with nearly a thousand men. The Third Maryland counted only 290. (26)

The regiment began the campaign when it struck camp at Kane's Landing, Virginia, on June 13. It crossed the Potomac River on a pontoon bridge at Edward's Ferry on June 26. Four days later it entered Pennsylvania and camped at Littlestown for the night. On July 1, the regiment was detailed to guard the divisional ordnance train and did not arrive at Gettysburg until the next day.

The Third Maryland occupied a position on Culp's Hill throughout the day and was only lightly engaged. Late in the afternoon it was pulled out of the line with the rest of the division and sent to the Union left to repel Longstreet's attack. By the time it got there the damage had been repaired. The regiment returned to its original position well after nightfall, only to find it in the hands of the enemy. After a few rounds were exchanged in the dark, Colonel Sudsburg had his men fall back a safe distance to await the break of day. (27)

The regiment remained in a reserve position throughout the morning of July 3. At noon it advanced and retook its former position. Two hours later it was shifted to the center of the brigade's line, but soon returned once more to its original section of breastworks on the right. One company was thrown forward as skirmishers and exchanged fire with the enemy until the end of the battle. The regiment spent the glorious Fourth of July collecting arms and burying the dead. (28) Casualties for the Third Maryland were mercifully light. One officer, Captain Henry Fenton of Company G, was killed and five enlisted men were wounded. Fenton enlisted on August 5, 1861 and had just been promoted to captain on May 18. (29)

The only battery of Maryland artillery with the Union Army at Gettysburg was Battery A, First Light Artillery, commanded by Captain James H. Rigby. The battery was originally part of the Purnell Legion and was transferred to the artillery reserve of the Army of the Potomac in the spring of 1862. At the time of the battle it was part of the Fourth Volunteer Brigade commanded by Captain Robert H. Fitzhugh. (30)

Rigby's Battery was detached to support the Twelfth Corps on the morning of July 2. It took up a position or, in the words of an artilleryman, "went into battery" on Powers Hill near the Baltimore Pike. Its first fire mission was Confederate batteries at a range of

Captain James H. Rigby.
Battery A, 1st Light Artillery. USA.

2500 yards. Rigby let loose with his 6 ten-pounder rifled guns at 2 p.m. After observing the effect of a few rounds, he judged the range too great to be effective and gave the order to cease fire. (31)

At first light on the morning of July 3, Captain Rigby received orders to shell the Confederate infantry on Culp's Hill. His men stood to their guns for several hours and fired over 200 rounds of Schenkle and Hotchkiss explosive shells. Rigby took 4 officers and 102 enlisted men into the battle and suffered no casualties. (32)

The last Maryland regiment to arrive at Gettysburg on July 2, and the one with the greatest odyssey, was the First Eastern Shore Infantry. Fearing that the Confederate victory at Manassas would rekindle the secession movement in the state, three prominent citizens wrote Governor Thomas H. Hicks a letter in August of 1861 requesting the formation of a regiment to serve on the Eastern Shore in the same fashion as the Potomac Home Brigade was being raised in Western Maryland at that time. By the end of the month the Secretary of War had authorized the regiment and James Wallace was appointed its colonel. (33)

On September 14, a seed of discontent was sown when Colonel Wallace received the following communication from the Assistant Secretary of War:

A Union battery in action at Gettysburg.

"Sir: You are hereby authorized to say to the men whom you propose to enlist in your regiment that they shall be used as a homeguard, stationed on the Eastern Shore of Maryland." (34)

That same month the First Eastern Shore Infantry was mustered into Federal Service at Cambridge to serve for three years. It was placed in General Henry H. Lockwood's brigade which originally consisted of the First and Second Eastern Shore regiments, Smith's Independent Company of Cavalry and Company A of the Purnell Legion Cavalry. (35)

On the eve of the Gettysburg Campaign, Lockwood commanded the First Separate Brigade of the Eighth Army Corps. His units were dispersed throughout Southern Maryland, the Eastern Shore, and the state of Delaware. When he received orders to concentrate his brigade and join the Army of the Potomac, all elements of his command complied except 61 men of Company K, First Eastern Shore Infantry, who held fast to the enlistment promise to serve exclusively on the Eastern Shore of Maryland. To their credit, 30 men of the company under Captain Littleton Long showed their patriotism by marching with the regiment as ordered.

Major General Schenck, the Department Commander of Maryland, ordered Second Lieutenant William J. Parker of Company K to disarm the men at their camp in Cambridge and dishonorably dismiss them from Federal service. Once transportation had been provided for the men to their homes, Lieutenant Parker was to join the balance of his company in the field. (36)

By June 23, 600 men of the First Eastern Shore Infantry had been consolidated near Baltimore City. After being issued new weapons, the regiment received orders on June 28 to join Lockwood's Brigade at Monocacy Bridge. The regiment marched as far as Ellicott Mills that day, where it received a warm welcome from the patriotic citizens of that town. A day long march brought the First to Poplar Springs where it went into camp. No sooner had the Eastern Shoremen cooked their rations and prepared for a well-earned night's rest than a cavalryman rode into camp with the startling news that Confederate cavalry were between them and Baltimore! This was Stuart with three brigades of cavalry and the wagon train he had captured near Rockville.

Duvall's company of Purnell Legion Cavalry had skirmished with the enemy and then joined the First Eastern Shore along with Rank's two cannons for mutual defense. If Stuart's veterans descended on the Union camp en masse, there was little doubt that they could be beaten off. Despite the odds, the infantry and artillery were placed on high ground

Asst. Surg. A. L. Manning.
1st Eastern Shore Infantry. USA.

Pvt. Robert H. Turner.
1st Eastern Shore Infantry. USA.

and the cavalry ordered to form a picket line. Fortunately, contact was made with Kilpatrick's Federal cavalry at Ridgeville and the two forces united before the Confederates could launch a successful attack. After a brief skirmish Stuart broke off the engagement and continued in the direction of Westminster.

At noon on June 30, the First Eastern Shore resumed its march with new orders to join Lockwood at Taneytown. It arrived there the next day and found General Meade's headquarters and news that the brigade was with the Twelfth Corps at Gettysburg. On the morning of July 2 the regiment stripped for action, leaving all excess baggage and sick men behind in camp. Setting off for the point of conflict, it reached Gettysburg at 6 p.m., but did not find Lockwood's Brigade on Culp's Hill until after nightfall. (37)

As Maryland Unionists and thousands of other Federal troops moved into position on Culp's Hill throughout July 2, the men of the First Maryland Battalion C.S.A. marveled at their own inactivity. The lowest private knew that with every passing hour the Federal lines were being made stronger. During the afternoon Longstreet launched his long awaited attack that caught General Dan Sickel's Third Corps near the Peach Orchard and immortalized two geographic formations known as Devil's Den and Little Round Top. The pressure of this attack caused General Meade to shift part of the Twelfth Corps from Culp's Hill to his threatened left flank. This had the effect of thinning out the Union lines that the First Maryland Battalion would soon attack.

At about 3 p.m. General Johnson asked Major Goldsborough to reconnoiter Benner's Hill as a possible position from which Major Latimer's guns could deliver a bombardment on the Union lines prior to an all out infantry attack. Goldsborough reported that the guns could fire on Culp's Hill with good effect, but that they would be open to a devastating fire from Cemetery Hill. Johnson overruled the objection and ordered Latimer into action. The infantry major feared for the safety of his fellow Marylanders in Andrews' Battalion. (38)

The artillery battalion had marched from Chambersburg on July 1 and arrived at Gettysburg just before sunset. It was temporarily under the command of nineteen-year-old Major Joseph W. Latimer. Despite his youth he was an excellent artillery officer of the same caliber as "The Gallant Pelham" and was referred to by his men as "The Boy Major." Andrews had been wounded in the arm during the fighting at Stevenson's Depot on June 14 and was forced to relinquish command of the battalion just before it crossed the Potomac River. (39)

It was mid-afternoon before Latimer received orders to place his guns on Benner's Hill. The hill straddled the Hanover Road just east of the town. It was mostly under cultivation with hardly a tree or a rock to protect the men while they served their guns. Latimer found the Rockbridge Artillery already in position on the north side of the Hanover Road with 4 twenty-pounder Parrott rifles. He ordered the section of like guns from the Lee Battery to stay north of the road with the other long range guns. Then he took the rest of the battalion across the road and went into battery on the south side. (40)

The remaining section of the Lee Battery, under the command of Captain C. I. Raine, was posted on the left of the line. Next came Captain William F. Dement's First Maryland, Captain J. C. Carpenter's Allegheny Artillery, and Captain William D. Brown's Fourth Maryland on the right next to the road. During the engagement Major Latimer assumed command of all Confederate artillery on Benner's Hill. Nearest the enemy he had 6 Napoleons, 3 three-inch rifles, and 5 ten-pounder Parrotts. On the far side of the road were 6 twenty-pounder Parrotts giving him a total of 20 pieces of artillery. Additional Confederate batteries lined Seminary Ridge, but were matched almost gun for gun by Union batteries on Cemetery Hill. Once Latimer gave the order to open fire, Benner's Hill would be the target area for over 40 pieces of Federal artillery. (41)

About 4 o'clock in the afternoon "The Boy Major" gave the fateful command to commence firing. The first rounds had barely cleared their tubes when the hilltop began to shake from the impact of solid shot and exploding shells. On Cemetery Hill 10 rifled guns from the Eleventh Corps opened fire from the west side of the Baltimore Pike in Evergreen Cemetery. On the east side of the pike Colonel Charles S. Wainwright commanded the First Corps artillery. He had been given ample time by the late attacking Confederates to put 23 pieces of artillery into position. His 10 Napoleons were excellent antipersonnel weapons when firing canister and 13 rifled guns equally effective at counter-battery fire. All but six of his pieces could reach Benner's Hill. Shortly after the Confederates opened fire, five additional guns from the Twelfth Corps on Culp's Hill joined the duel as did Rigby's Battery from the artillery reserve. (42)

The First Maryland Artillery contained a large number of men from Southern Maryland and Baltimore City. Richard Snowden Andrews convinced members of the Charles County Mounted Volunteers to form an artillery unit when they arrived in Richmond in 1861. Andrews was elected the first captain of the battery. He was replaced by Lieutenant Dement when promoted to major. The First Maryland was assigned to the battalion in the spring of 1863 and the battalion to Johnson's Division just before the campaign began. (43)

Dave Mark

Pvt. Addison Cook.
1st MD Artillery. CSA.

As both sides exchanged salvos, Dement's Battery lost a limber to Copper's Pennsylvania battery on Cemetery Hill; or more precisely, to the carelessness of one of its men. Corporal Samuel Hatton was responsible for removing ammunition from the limber chest so that it could be carried up to the gun. After each round was withdrawn he was to close the copper-sheathed lid tightly so that flying sparks would not cause an explosion. This he failed to do more than once. When warned by a fellow gunner he replied, "Oh nothing is going to hurt Sam . . . ." A few seconds later a shell exploded overhead, dropping sparks into the open chest. This touched off an explo-

Capt. William D. Brown.
4th MD Artillery. CSA.

sion which reduced the limber to a pile of rubble and sent Sam flying to the ground a scorched corpse. (44)

Over on Cemetery Hill Lieutenant James Stewart of the Regular Artillery saw the flash and smoke of the explosion and ordered his men to give three cheers for the Pennsylvania volunteers. This was immediately followed by a round from the Rockbridge Artillery that struck one of Stewart's caissons and launched three ammunition chests skyward. (45)

The Fourth Maryland Artillery was known as the Chesapeake Artillery. Most of its men came from Saint Mary's County and Baltimore City. Attached to Andrews' Battalion since the Peninsular Campaign, it was armed with 4 ten-pounder Parrotts taken from Cushing's Battery at the battle of Cedar Mountain in August of 1862. When Major Latimer gave the order to open fire, Captain William D. Brown rode to the front of the battery and exhorted his men to stand by the guns for the honor of their state. As he spoke a solid shot struck his right leg, passed through the belly of the horse and broke his left leg. The horse sank to the ground like a hulled ship breaking three of Brown's ribs and covering him with gore. (46)

Lieutenant Walter S. Chew was now in command of the Fourth Maryland or what was left of it. Three of the four pieces were soon out of action. Corporal Daniel Dougherty was cut in half by an incoming round. Private Jack Brain and Private Fred Cusick were both decapitated. When Private Jacob Cook went in search of ammunition for his gun he saw a shell explode in front of the lead pair of the limber team, killing both horses and disemboweling the driver, Private Thaddeus Parker. Others suffered less gruesome injuries.

At one point the firing fell off on both sides, possibly from mutual exhaustion. Lieutenant Chew shifted his able-bodied men to the one remaining piece that was still in service. Latimer ordered the battery to open fire for a second time. The Union response was equally swift and devastating. No sooner had Private Cook loaded a charge than an incoming round struck the right wheel of his piece, breaking it and wounding four more members of the crew. Lieutenant Benjamin G. Roberts was mortally wounded while commanding the section. (47)

Facing annihilation, Latimer sent his sergeant major to General Johnson to inform him that the battalion could not stay in action much longer. The general approved the removal of all but four guns. These were to remain on Benner's Hill and support the infantry attack that was about to be launched. Major Latimer supervised the withdrawal of his wounded men and damaged equipment. Then he returned to the remaining four guns and ordered them to commence firing for the third and final time. The Union artillery renewed its shower of deadly iron. A shell exploded near "The Boy Major," tearing into his arm and killing his horse. With Latimer down Captain Raine assumed command of the battalion for the remainder of the battle.

Raine pulled the last four guns off the hill under the cover of darkness on July 2. The next day he was ordered to park near an ordnance train and resupply his limber chests. The battalion took no part in the massive artillery bombardment that preceded Picket's Charge. That evening it was ordered to the front to guard against a counterattack if one should come. On the night of July 4, the battalion fell in with the army as it commenced its retreat to Virginia. Andrews, not yet fully recovered himself, met the mortally wounded Latimer at Hagerstown,

Maryland, and resumed command of the battalion. The young officer's arm had been amputated, but the effects of the wound were such that he died on the first of August.

After he returned to Virginia, Andrews wrote his official report for the battalion during the battle. He stated that the unit had 3 officers wounded, 10 enlisted men killed, and 32 wounded. Also lost were 30 horses. Two caissons were destroyed and one limber chest damaged. Latimer's guns had fired a total of 1147 rounds.

The First Maryland Artillery had 1 corporal killed and 10 enlisted men wounded. One caisson exploded and one was damaged, and 9 horses were lost. In the Chesapeake Artillery both Captain Dement and Lieutenant Benjamin Roberts died from the wounds they received on Benner's Hill. The battery also had six enlisted men killed, eight wounded, and lost half of its horses. (48)

Johnson's Division consisted of four infantry brigades: Nicholl's with five Louisiana regiments, the Stonewall Brigade with five, Jones Brigade with six Virginia regiments, and Steuart's Brigade.

George Hume "Maryland" Steuart was born in Baltimore City in 1828. He graduated from West Point in 1847 and was commissioned a lieutenant in the Second Dragoons. He resigned his commission in April of 1861 and became lieutenant colonel of the First Maryland Infantry Regiment. After the first Battle of Bull Run he was promoted to colonel of the regiment, then brigadier general in March of 1862. Steuart commanded a brigade in General Ewell's Division during the Valley Campaign until he was wounded in the shoulder at the Battle of Cross Keys.

After the Battle of Gettysburg, Steuart remained with the Army of Northern Virginia until he was captured with most of Johnson's Division at Spottsylvania in 1864. Exchanged later that year, he was given command of a brigade in Pickett's Division. Paroled at Appomattox, Steuart returned to his home in Anne Arundel County where he took up farming after the war. At one time he commanded the United Confederate Veterans Department of Maryland. Steuart is buried in Green Mount Cemetery in Baltimore.

Johnson's brigades waited behind Benner's Hill for the artillery to soften up the Union lines on Culp's Hill. Quite a few shells fired by the Yankees overshot their targets and landed among the prone infantry. At 7 p.m. their attack began with the remnant of Latimers' guns providing fire support. Their objective was to capture Culp's Hill and open the way for an attack on the rear of the Union line. (49)

Culp's Hill can best be described as a small shapeless hill joined to a larger one. The faces of both hills are covered with huge boulders and thickly wooded in places. The Union troops holding this position had spent the last 24 hours merging breastworks with rock formations to form a natural fortress. By the time the Confederate battle line had crossed Rock Creek and began to inch its way up the slopes of Culp's Hill it was completely dark. The only thing that favored the Rebel advance was the absence of the Twelfth Corps units that had been shifted to the Union left flank earlier in the day. This meant that there would be fewer Yankees to deal with if or when they reached the top of the hill.

The order of battle for Johnson's Division during the attack was Jone's Brigade on the right and Nicholl's Brigade in the center. Steuart's Brigade formed the left flank of both the division and the entire army during the attack on July 2. The Stonewall Brigade was back on Brinkerhoff's Ridge fending off an advance by Union cavalry that included the First Maryland Cavalry and Company A of the Purnell Legion. Johnson ordered Walker to repulse the cavalry and rejoin the division while the attack was in progress.

Steuart's Brigade went into action with the Third North Carolina and First Maryland on the right and the three Virginia regiments on the left. The First North Carolina followed in their wake as a reserve. As the brigade groped its way up hill, the Third North Carolina and First Maryland approached a line of breastworks it could not see in the dark. When they were within a few yards of the works, two New York regiments from General George S. Green's brigade fired a devastating volley into the front and flank of the unsuspecting Rebels. (50)

As the First Maryland slugged it out with the New Yorkers, Lieutenant Randolph McKim brought up eight companies of the First North Carolina to support the attack. Seeing muzzle flashes in his front and receiving minie balls that were overshooting the Confederate battle line, he mistakenly ordered his men to fire into the back of the First Maryland. The mistake was soon corrected when Major Parsely of the Third North Carolina rushed up screaming, "They are our own men...." (51)

The First North Carolina was then brought in line with the other two units and together they pushed forward to occupy the first line of Federal breastworks. In the charge Lt. Colonel James R. Herbert was wounded three times. Command of the battalion fell to Major Goldsborough. Goldsborough sensed that additional troops were being massed in his front. This was confirmed by a number of officers and men who wandered into his lines from different regiments. Fearing a counterattack, he positioned his men along the captured enemy works for the remaining hours of darkness. The firefight lasted until 11 p.m., with random shooting until daybreak. (52)

During the night attack of July 2, Early's Division struck the northeast slope of Cemetery Hill. The brigades of Hoke and Hays routed a

Lt. Randolph H. McKim.
Staff of Gen. Steuart. CSA.

number of Federal regiments and captured several batteries. One of the units sent to reinforce the Eleventh Corps was the Gibraltar Brigade commanded by Colonel Samuel Sprigg Carroll. Carroll was one of 45 Regular Army officers from Maryland who remained in Federal service when the war began. He was the highest ranking Marylander in blue at Gettysburg and the only one in the battle to later attain the rank of general, that coming in 1864. Carroll's brigade recaptured Rickett's Battery and drove the Confederate infantry back down the hill. (53)

Dave Mark

Lt. Col. James R. Herbert.
1st MD Battalion. CSA.

JULY 3, 1863

Before any offensive operations could be undertaken by Johnson's Division on July 3, General A.S. Williams ordered the Twelfth Corps artillery to rake the line of breastworks on Culp's Hill captured by the Rebels the night before. Twenty-six guns from Muhlenberg's Brigade

Maj. W. W. Goldsborough.
1st MD Battalion. CSA.

Col. Samuel S. Carroll.
Eleventh Corps. USA.

and Rigby's Maryland battery opened a barrage on the unsuspecting infantry. Three companies of the First Battalion had advanced past the safety of the earthworks during the night. Caught in a storm of shot and shell, they quickly bounded back to the leeward side of the fortifications. At 8 o'clock Goldsborough paid a visit to Company A on the right of the line. Captain William Murray reported heavy casualties and a scarcity of ammunition. Lieutenant McKim immediately volunteered to secure the needed rounds. He took three men and moved back down the slope while under the fire of enemy sharpshooters. The detail soon located a supply train and returned with two boxes of cartridges. (54)

Johnson was ordered to resume his attack against Culp's Hill on July 3 to prevent General Meade from reinforcing his center when Pickett's grand assault was launched against Cemetery Ridge. The Stonewall Brigade would continue to attack the upper part of Culp's Hill while Steuart's Brigade would hit the northwest slope of the lower hill.

When General Steuart's staff officer delivered the order to Major Goldsborough to form up with the Virginia regiments on his left for a final assault, he exclaimed "...it was nothing less than murder to send men into that slaughter pen." Captain Williams agreed and made known General Steuart's disapproval as well. Murray, as senior captain, was

Captain William H. Murray.
1st MD Battalion. CSA.

given command of the right of the battalion. Goldsborough would go into battle on the left. The First Maryland was on the very right of the brigade's line of battle. (55)

Captain Murray was well thought of by his men. He had served from the very beginning of the war with the original First Maryland and recruited the first company in the new battalion. Realizing the hopelessness of the task, he shook the hand of every man in his company and said, "Good-bye, it is not likely that we shall meet again." (56)

General Steuart took position just behind Company A of his beloved Marylanders. Word was passed to fix bayonets. Then the general drew his sword and ordered "Attention! Forward, double-quick! March!" Murray, in turn, raised his sword and led his men forward for the last time. Their objective was the Union line of earthworks that lay about 200 yards away on the other side of an open field. As the advancing infantry cleared the tree line it immediately came under a crossfire from both musket and cannon. The One Hundred and Forty-Seventh Pennsylvania Regiment delivered a volley at the range of 100 yards with devastating effect on the advancing Marylanders. (57)

Despite the unrelenting Union musketry, Captain Murray continued to lead Company A closer and closer to the enemy works until he was mortally wounded. As his brother Alex rushed to catch the falling William, he was struck by an exploding shell and knocked unconscious. A third brother, Lieutenant Clapham Murray, then assumed command of the Murray Company.

On the left Goldsborough advanced through "... a merciless storm of bullets..." until shot from his horse. Two companies of Marylanders and 18 North Carolinians advanced to within 50 yards of the Union line when the Twenty-Ninth Pennsylvania Infantry volleyed on them with deadly effect. A few of the men charged independently into the breastworks where they died among their enemy.

Pvt. Alexander Murray. 1st MD Battalion. CSA.

By now several of the Union regiments had used up their ammunition and were replaced with men from William's division, including the First Potomac Home Brigade, the Third Maryland Infantry, and the newly arrived First Eastern Shore Regiment.

When the First Potomac Home Brigade returned to Culp's Hill on the night of July 2, it wandered into a firefight between the attacking Confederates in the first line of works and the Union troops holding the second line further up the hill. Colonel Maulsby could not distinguish friend from foe in the darkness and wisely moved his men back to Cemetery Hill where they slept with the artillery until summoned the next morning. As fate would have it the regiment was sent to relieve the Twenty-Ninth Pennsylvania which has just emptied its muskets into the ranks of the First Maryland Battalion. (58)

Maulsby received orders to attack the stone wall behind which the Maryland Confederates had sought shelter. Leaving the safety of their

Lt. Col. John A. Steiner.
1st Potomac Home Brigade. USA.

works these Marylanders in blue advanced to within 30 yards of their objective. Colonel Maulsby ordered his men to halt and fix bayonets before going in for the final strike against their former friends and neighbors. At this critical moment the regiment was ordered to pull back and the terrible consequences of their charge were avoided. The affair was still costly for the regiment. In action for only half an hour it had lost nearly 100 men. One of those who survived was Major Roger E. Cook who stood only five feet tall. The man directly behind him was killed. Cook credited his survival to his short stature. (59)

Lt. Colonel John A. Steiner commanded the left of the line during the charge. Steiner had tendered his resignation to take effect on June 12, 1863. When the regiment received orders to join the Army of the Potomac, he voluntarily remained on duty until the campaign ended. He officially resigned at Sandy Hook, Maryland, on July 16 having kept his promise not to leave the Army until the rebels were driven out of Maryland and Pennsylvania. Steiner became the sheriff of Frederick in November of 1863. On March 13, 1865, he received the rank of brevet brigadier general, for faithful and meritorious service. (60)

The First Potomac Home Brigade fell back to the turnpike but was out of action less than an hour when Major General Henry W. Slocum passed by leading the First Eastern Shore to the front. The attack by Johnson's Division was still under way and more men were needed to hold the line. Maulsby's regiment was sent to reinforce General Green's brigade, where it remained until the end of the fighting on Culp's Hill. During the height of Pickett's Charge, General Slocum ordered Lockwood's Brigade to reinforce the Union center. The First Potomac Home Brigade was again pulled out of the works and marched toward another possible breakthrough. Before the column could reach the point of danger, a staff officer brought the welcome news that the attack had been repulsed. (61)

At 8 o'clock in the morning of July 3, the First Eastern Shore Infantry was ordered to the front for its baptism of fire. It consisted of 500 men in nine companies. The battle had been raging for hours when the novice regiment crossed the Baltimore Pike to join the fighting on Culp's Hill. Scarred rocks and broken trees were added to the grim scene of dead and dying soldiers. (62)

As the First Eastern Shore Infantry approached the rear of the line held by a Pennsylvania regiment, it began to feel the effects of Confederate small arms fire. In the confusion of their first battle, Lt. Colonel Comegys took four companies to the left while Colonel Wallace led the remaining five directly toward the Union breastworks. As he reached the crest of the hill, he saw the oncoming Rebels and ordered his men to open fire over the heads of the Pennsylvanians. The combined firepower of the two units drove off the assault. With empty cartridge boxes the Pennsylvania regiment turned over the works to Wallace's part of the regiment. Here they remained for two hours until they too were out of ammunition and in turn relieved by the One Hundred and Fiftieth New York. By the end of the day the First Eastern Shore had 7 men killed, 22 wounded, and 7 missing. (63)

Lt. James T. Smith. Co. C.
1st Potomac Home Brigade. K.I.A.

From prisoners taken it was soon learned that the First Eastern Shore Infantry U.S. had been fighting with at least part of the First Maryland Infantry Battalion C.S. Of even greater coincidence was the fact that the color bearer of Company H, First Eastern Shore Infantry, Sergeant Robert W. Ross, was the cousin of Color Sergeant P.M. Moore of Company E in the First Maryland Battalion! Ross survived the battle unharmed. Moore was wounded four times and captured by his friends and neighbors from Talbot County. (64)

As the First Maryland hovered on the edge of extinction, a small dog, the mascot of the battalion, charged into the Union lines and returned limping to his comrades. After the battle the dog was found lying with a dead Confederate soldier "perfectly riddled" with gunshot wounds. General Thomas L. Kane of the Twelfth Corps ordered the dog to be buried with honors.

As survivors of the ill-fated charge fell back to the safety of the stone wall they had captured the night before, General Steuart wept openly and cried out, "My poor boys! My poor boys!" During the retreat Lieutenant J. Winder Laird found Major Goldsborough lying on the ground. He picked up the wounded officer and carried him to safety. When they were within the Confederate lines Goldsborough issued orders for Captain Murray to assume command of the battalion. It was only then that he learned of Murray's death and command passed to Captain J. Parran Crane. (65)

The First Maryland remained behind the stone wall for about an hour shielding itself from incoming Union fire. Then, gathering as many of the wounded as possible, it made its way back down the slope of Culp's Hill and crossed to the east bank of Rock Creek where it stayed until 11:30 that night. Randolph McKim estimated the losses of the battalion at 206 men. Lt. Colonel Herbert reported 250. Company A, the Murray Company, lost 18 men killed and 37 wounded out of 97 present for duty. (66)

All along the line the Confederates were unsuccessful in their attempts to capture Culp's Hill. Johnson's adjutant, Henry Kyd Douglas, volunteered to lead two regiments of Smith's Brigade to the aid of Steuart's men. En route they relieved the Second Virginia Infantry that was acting as a flank guard for the Stonewall Brigade. In the Second Virginia was a man named Wesley Culp. Wesley had left his home near the town of Gettysburg to work as a carriage maker in Shepherdstown, Virginia. When the war broke out he stayed south and enlisted in Company B, which was commanded at the time by then-Captain Douglas. Because Culp was so short, Douglas procured for him a special downsized musket. The Second Virginia joined the Stonewall Brigade in its attack on the upper section of Culp's Hill. It was during this action that Wesley Culp was killed within sight of the house where he was born.

After the brief encounter with his old command, Douglas continued to lead Smith's regiments toward the front. Several of the men in the ranks warned Douglas to dismount, but he considered it inappropriate for a staff officer to do so. As Douglas drew his sword and pointed to the area he wished the infantry to occupy, a line of Yankee skirmishers opened fire, wounding him. He managed to keep to his saddle until some nearby infantry officers could help him to the ground. The ball had entered his left shoulder carrying a piece of his coat, shirt, and undershirt with it. As the brigade battle line passed by, General Smith

Maj. Henry Kyd Douglas.
Staff of Gen. Johnson. CSA.

stopped to express his concern for the wounded major and then hastened on to join his command.

Douglas was more fortunate than most of the battle casualties at Gettysburg. He was carried to the rear and then transported to a house on the Hunterstown Road where he was placed on the parlor floor. No less than six surgeons stopped to examine the man who once rode with Stonewall Jackson. When Lee's army retreated, Douglas was left behind with a barn full of wounded Rebels under the care of Surgeon Taney.

During his period of convalescence the major was cared for by the Picking family, in whose home he was staying, and Smith Shepherd of Company B, who gave up his freedom to look after his old company

DCT

Capt. Gustavus W. Dorsey.
Co. K. 1st VA Cavalry. CSA.

commander. In a few days Douglas's mother and sister arrived from his home along the Potomac River. They had driven their carriage through the lines of both armies during the Confederate retreat from Gettysburg.

In mid-July the wounded major was transferred to the Seminary Hospital where he found General Trimble and others who were not able to make it back to "Old Virginia." When sufficiently recovered he was sent to a military hospital in Baltimore and then on to Point Lookout. Exchanged the following year, Douglas served in the Army of Northern Virginia until its surrender at Appomattox. When he returned home after the war he joined the Maryland National Guard, as did many other Civil War veterans. Douglas was promoted to State Adjutant General and commanded the Guard from 1892 to 1896. (67)

The second phase of Lee's plan called for J.E.B. Stuart's cavalry, which had arrived late on the night of July 2, to pass around the Confederate left flank and attack the rear of the Union line. This would give him the opportunity to capture the massive Federal wagon trains in that area and divert reinforcements away from the planned breakthrough on Cemetery Hill. Within the cavalry division were several groups of Marylanders.

As mentioned before, the First Maryland Cavalry had been detached from Fitzhugh Lee's Brigade and was serving with Ewell's corps. In the same brigade was Company K of the First Virginia Regiment. The company originally consisted of 75 men, mostly from Howard and Montgomery Counties. They were mustered into the First Virginia as Company M in August of 1861. When then-Colonel Fitzhugh Lee took command of the regiment in 1862, he changed the unit designation to Company K so that it could serve in the coveted position of "Right Company" in the regimental formation. In 1864 the company transferred to the First Maryland Cavalry and its captain, Gustavus W. Dorsey, took command of the battalion for the remainder of the war. (68)

Also serving with the Cavalry Division of the Army of Northern Virginia were six batteries of light guns known as The Stuart Horse Artillery. One of the batteries was commanded by Captain James Breathed of Washington County, Maryland. Although designated a Virginia battery, Breathed's command contained over 100 Marylanders including 10 officers. (69) Another horse artillery unit was the Second Maryland, or Baltimore Light Artillery, commanded by Captain William H. Griffin. The Second Maryland had distinguished itself at the battle of Winchester and General John B.

Gordon rewarded it by allowing Griffin to refit his battery with the best pieces captured from the Yankees. Thus the battery entered the battle with a full complement of Parrott guns—possibly the same guns captured from their counterpart in the Union Army, Alexander's Maryland battery, which had been defending the Star Fort. The Baltimore Light accompanied Jenkin's Brigade of cavalry in the vanguard of the Army of Northern Virginia as it marched toward Gettysburg. (70)

Stuart moved his cavalry three miles east of Gettysburg and

Dave Mark

Sgt. N. C. Hobbs.
Co. K. 1st VA Cavalry. CSA.

Dave Mark

Capt. James Breathed.
Stuart Horse Artillery. CSA.

occupied Cress's Ridge. From there he could cover the left flank of
Ewell's corps and at the same time be in a position to attack the Union
rear. Simultaneously, the two brigades of Gregg's Cavalry Division were
ordered to cover the right flank of the Union line east of Culp's Hill.
This put them on a collision course with the Rebel cavalry. First contact
was made by White's Battalion moving along the York Road.

   With the massive artillery barrage pounding in the distance, Stuart
ordered a portion of Jenkins' Brigade to dismount and advance a skirmish line on foot. Jenkins' men were in fact mounted infantry armed
with Enfied muskets. This gave them an advantage over the short range
Union carbines until their limited supply of ammunition was expended.

   Gregg determined to disrupt the Confederate advance before it
could build momentum by forming his own line of skirmishers. He sent
the Third Pennsylvania and First Maryland Regiments forward, sup-

Capt. William H. Griffin.
Second MD Artillery. CSA.

ported by the First New Jersey Artillery. A little after 2 p.m., the Union skirmishers struck a fence line in front of the Rummel barn held by Jenkins' men. Company A of the Purnell Legion was in the line next to two companies of the Third Pennsylvania. Rebel sharpshooters used the barn to advantage until the Union horse artillery drove them out. Gregg committed more men and extended the Union line to the left of the Purnell Legion company. (71)

At the time General Gregg took up a position along the Hanover Pike, he was warned by General George Armstrong Custer to expect an attack by Confederate cavalry. Gregg kept Custer's brigade of four Michigan regiments to increase his division's strength. When Stuart's advance stalled, he ordered a saber charge by the brigades of Fitzhugh Lee and Wade Hampton which temporarily sent the Purnell Legion and the rest of the Union line rearward. Gregg ordered General Custer to lead his "Wolverines" in a counterattack supported by both brigades of his division. The two mounted forces collided like runaway locomotives. The Confederates were stopped and then pushed back to Cress's Ridge. Company A of the Purnell Legion fell in with their adopted brigade and

Lt. Col. James M. Deems.
1st MD Cavalry. USA.

Sgt. Henry Glunt. Co. G.
1st MD Cavalry. USA.

helped with the counterattack. (72) Lt. Colonel James M. Deems was ordered to take the First Maryland Cavalry Regiment to cover the extreme right flank of the Union line. Casualties were light for the Maryland horsemen. The First Regiment had two officers and seven enlisted men wounded and one man missing. Company A of the Legion reported no losses. (73)

The final glory for both armies at Gettysburg was Pickett's Charge. General Lee had assailed both flanks of the Union Army with infantry and attempted to gain its rear with Stuart's cavalry. All his efforts were turned back by equally heroic actions on the part of the Federal forces. Not ready to settle for a draw, Lee ordered one more attack on July 3. Colonel E. Porter Alexander was ordered to amass 170 cannon on Seminary Ridge with the expressed purpose of pulverizing the center of the Union line on Cemetery Hill. This was to be followed by a massive infantry assault led by General George E. Pickett's Division supported

Dave Mark

Major Osmond Latrobe.
Staff of Gen. Longstreet. CSA.

by those of Heth and Trimble—in all, some ten to fifteen thousand men. At the center of the target area General Henry Hunt, Meade's Chief of Artillery, waited with 77 guns. Over twice that number were within supporting distance. (74)

Longstreet's First Corps was also sprinkled with Marylanders, both as officers and soldiers in the ranks. Major Osmond Latrobe served on the staff of General Longstreet and was sited "For valuable and meritous service on the field" in the general's official report after the battle. (75)

One of the brigades in Pickett's Division was commanded by Brigadier General Lewis A. Armistead. Born in North Carolina, he was the nephew of Major George Armistead who commanded the garrison at Fort McHenry during the famous bombardment that gave birth to our National Anthem in 1814. In his brigade was Company B, Ninth Virginia Infantry composed of Maryland men who had enlisted in that regiment in 1861. Armistead managed to lead a fragment of his brigade across the stone wall to the legendary "high water mark" of the Confederacy. As he laid his hand on one of the Union cannon to signify its capture, he was mortally wounded and died two days later. His body was claimed by his father and taken to Baltimore where it was placed in the tomb of Major Armistead. He was later buried at Saint Paul's Episcopal Church. (76)

Commanding Pender's Division during the charge was Major General Isaac Ridgeway Trimble, the third and highest ranking Marylander

Maj. Gen. Isaac R. Trimble. CSA.

general in gray at Gettysburg. Although born in Virginia, Trimble took up residence in Maryland in 1832 after ten years service in the Regular Army. His engineering skills learned at West Point were put to use on the Baltimore and Susquehanna Railroad. A mark of his acceptance in the state was his being given command of the 10,000 man "Un-uni-formed Volunteer Corps" which was formed immediately after the Pratt Street Riot in Baltimore City in April of 1861. Two months later he returned to Virginia and was appointed brigadier general. He served in Jackson's corps until wounded at the Battle of Groverton in 1862. Early in 1863 he was promoted to major general on the recommendation of both Lee and Jackson. (77)

When Trimble arrived at Gettysburg he was a supernumerary in the Second Corps. He made a personal reconnaissance of the Union position on July 1, and unsuccessfully urged Ewell to attack at once. Dissatisfied with Ewell as a corps commander and thirsting for action, he reported to Lee's headquarters when he learned the army had lost two division commanders. The 61-year-old general was given command of two brigades from Pender's Division which were already forming for the charge. Fortunately, Trimble had a reputation as a fighter—there would be no time for formal introductions. Lee and Trimble inspected the brigades of Lane and Scale. Then Lee rode off muttering, "The attack must succeed." (78)

At a little past 3 p.m., the Confederate battering ram moved off across a mile of open fields with Pickett's Division on the right and Heth's Division on the left, followed by Trimble's newly acquired command. When Trimble reached the Emmitsburg Road he stopped to organize his men for the final length of the charge. As he sat on his mare Jinny, a musket ball struck his left leg and penetrated through to the horse. Barely able to keep to his saddle, he sent word to General Lane to assume command of the division. Lane pushed the North Carolina regiments to within yards of the stone wall before the attack was finally broken. The wounded horse and rider stood like an island in the receding tide of the great charge. (79)

Trimble managed to regain the Confederate lines, but the wound cost him his leg. Left behind when the army retreated, he was taken prisoner on July 5 with many other Rebels whose injuries prohibited the long journey back to Virginia. Trimble was moved to a warehouse owned by Robert McCurdy, the president of the Gettysburg Railroad. McCurdy, possibly a prewar associate in the railroad business, personally cared for the wounded general.

After a period of convalescence, Trimble was transferred to the prisoner of war camp at Johnson's Island. He was exchanged in April of 1865 for generals Crook and Kelly who had been captured in a raid on Cumberland, Maryland, in February of the same year. By the time he reached Virginia the war was over and he returned to Baltimore City. He died there in 1888 at the age of 86. (80)

Cemetery Ridge after Pickett's Charge. From a war-time sketch.

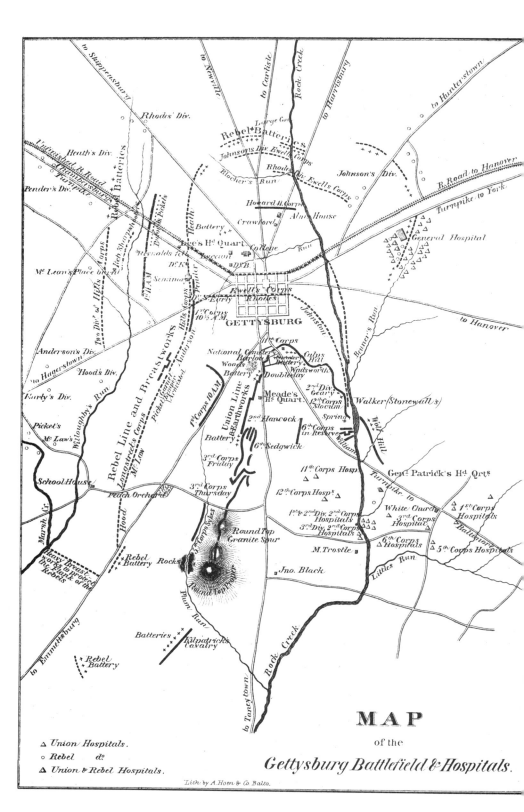

MAP

of the

Gettysburg Battlefield & Hospitals.

△ Union Hospitals.
○ Rebel do.
▲ Union & Rebel Hospitals.

Lith. by A. Hoen & Co Balto.

Chapter 2

THE AFTERMATH

Lee's army moved off under the cover of darkness on the night of July 4, leaving behind thousands of wounded and unburied dead. General Meade held most of his army in place throughout the next day. He wanted to determine if Lee was really headed for the Potomac River or simply maneuvering for another battle. To this end he sent the relatively fresh Sixth Corps on a reconnaissance across the Emmitsburg Pike early on the morning of July 5. Crossing through what had been "no man's land" for the previous three days, the Union Infantry occupied Lee's abandoned line on Seminary Ridge. By mid-morning the entire battlefield of Gettysburg was in the hands of the Union Army. It was an endless field of death and destruction. (1)

With the exodus of the Rebels, a new army descended on the town of Gettysburg. It was filled with doctors and nurses, volunteers and scavengers, relatives seeking loved ones and soldiers detailed to clean up the battlefield. They came from many different states and many different organizations with backgrounds that ranged from religious order to high society.

The first contingent to arrive from Maryland was 14 members of the Sisters of Charity, led by Father Francis Burlando. The priest and nuns were from Saint Joseph's Academy in Emmitsburg, a small town just south of the state line where they ran a convent and nationally recognized boarding school for girls. The nuns had fed soldiers from both armies during the week before the battle. The residents of Saint Joseph's clearly heard the sounds of the battle for three days. On the night of July 4 they learned from Rebel soldiers that the battle was over and Lee was headed south.

The next day Father Burlando and the good sisters set out for Gettysburg in the school's carriage and wagon. With them they brought food and medical supplies for the wounded. Before reaching their objective, the small caravan was halted by Union pickets. Father

Burlando left the carriage and advanced toward the soldiers with a white handkerchief tied to the end of his cane. Once the priest had explained the noble purpose of their mission the soldiers quickly lowered their weapons and pulled open a barricade of trees from the road. As the party passed through, the soldiers lifted their caps and bowed in appreciation for the aid that was about to be given their comrades.

Soon the horrors of the battlefield were revealed to these Soldiers of Christ. Burned out buildings, dead horses and abandoned military equipment covered the ground in all directions. The course of the wagons had to be continuously adjusted to avoid the strewn bodies of soldiers from both armies. Father Burlando later wrote:

> "The further we advanced, the more abundant were the evidences presented to our eyes of the terrible conflict, and tears could not be restrained . . ."

One of the nuns in the party, Sister Matilda, also wrote of her first impression of war.

> "O! This picture of human beings slaughtered down by their fellow men in a cruel civil war was perfectly awful. The battlefield a very extensive space on either side of the road . . . were men digging pits and putting the bodies down by the dozens."

When the party entered the town of Gettysburg, they were recognized by some of the soldiers they had fed the week before and received a hearty welcome. Moving through the congested streets, they soon came to the town square and set up their base of operation in the McClellan Hotel. After a quick tour of the surrounding buildings being used to house the wounded, which was just about every public building and church in the town, the sisters began to care for the wounded. Father Burlando stationed two of the nuns in each of the three main hospitals and six at the hotel. At the end of the day he returned to Emmitsburg with the remaining two nuns.

The next day Father Burlando returned with more help plus beds and blankets for the nuns who had been forced to sleep on the floor the night before. He also brought them a supply of hams, coffee, tea, and other food stuff. On July 7 their ranks were again increased by the arrival of sisters from the convent in Baltimore City. The Sisters of Charity worked throughout the hot summer days caring for the soldiers of both armies wherever the need was greatest. (2)

One of the largest and best organized groups of volunteers to aid the wounded soldiers at Gettysburg was the United States Christian Commission. Like its sister organization, the Sanitary Commission, it had learned many valuable lessons from their efforts to relieve the suffering after the Battle of Antietam in 1862. First and foremost was the fact that the United States Army, as it existed, could never care for large numbers of casualties with military personnel alone.

As soon as work of the battle reached the state, members of the Baltimore Committee of the Christian Commission began to organize a relief expedition. By July 3, Mr. J.B. Stillson and a group of men from the Commission were at Westminster, Maryland, waiting for their supply wagons to catch up with them. Major General Hancock and his aide, General Miller, were brought into the town at three o'clock the next morning. All army surgeons had been ordered to the front and Mr. Stillson personally cared for the two wounded generals before continuing on to the scene of the battle.

Mr. Louis Muller arrived in Gettysburg by train on July 8. The railroad bridge being burned, he was forced to unload his supplies about one mile from the town and haul them in three wagons to their base of operation at the square. Men from the Commission worked in squads of six or less. They would draw supplies from a central issuing point and carry them by foot or in wagons to the surrounding hospitals. Mr. Muller was put in charge of the "feeding department." On his first day he reported feeding 2000 soldiers in the town and an equal number in the field hospitals. (3)

Baltimoreans from all walks of life hastened to the battlefield to minister to the wounded of both armies. William McPhail and Company was joined by 10 men from the Number 4 Fire Department and Mr. Charles H. Keener, Esq., who was superintendent of the Maryland Institution for the Blind. Mr. Keener spent over five weeks at Gettysburg as a volunteer with the Christian Commission. He arrived on July 5 in company with an army photographer who helped steer him around Confederate cavalry patrols. This may well have been either Alexander Gardner or James Pyson; both were known to have taken photographs soon after the battle. Most of the time he worked in the Second Corps hospital dressing wounds. One case will suffice to illustrate the nature of this work.

> ". . . one of the Commission suggested to me to dress
> wounds. This I did for almost two weeks. constantly. I
> had not gone far before I met Mr. Luther White of the
> 20th Massachusetts, whose head was severely wounded

by a shell, a piece of which, 1¹/₂ inches square, was removed from the right side, and the skull trepanned. Nearly all the ear was gone, and the hearing and sight of that side destroyed, and when I first saw him the side of his head seemed to be a mass of ragged flesh and clotted blood. I never expected to see him alive a second time, but about a week after was hailed by him, as I passed through his tent."

By the 5th of August the Second Corps hospital was disbanded and the remaining patients transferred to the General Hospital. Keener moved with them and stayed on until August 14 when he returned to his duties at the institution. (4)

The Christian Commission in Baltimore continued to receive donations from citizens throughout the state without any stipulation as to which army's soldiers would benefit. By late August all the wounded that had not been shipped out were consolidated in two locations: the General Hospital located near the railroad and the Lutheran Theological Seminary. As hospitals opened in other locations, the Commission sent aid to Frederick, Annapolis, and Point Lookout. (5)

The saddest contingent of the "third army" at Gettysburg were those seeking their loved ones either lost in the battle or suffering in a field hospital. For relatives coming from one of the loyal states the cost of transportation was the biggest hurdle to overcome. For those from the deep South it was all but impossible. Marylanders seeking their kin, regardless of which side they had fought on, were at least fortunate to be near the battlefield and already within the Union lines.

As noted earlier, Major Henry Kyd Douglas was left behind in a private residence and soon joined by his mother and sister, who cared for him until he was shipped off to a Northern prison. The body of Captain William Murray, who had been killed on Culp's Hill, received extraordinary treatment. The men of his company must have buried him nearby and marked the spot well, for most Rebels were simply thrown into a common grave by Union soldiers assigned the disagreeable task. Some weeks after the battle, Murray's half-sister Elizabeth and a family servant made the trip in a wagon from southern Anne Arundel County to Gettysburg. The grave site was found and his remains removed to the cemetery behind Christ Church in Owensville, Maryland. All such proceedings did not receive universal abidance. The body of Captain William D. Brown, Chesapeake Artillery, was returned to Baltimore for burial in Green Mount Cemetery. After the graveside service was concluded on July 31, Colonel William S. Fish, the provost marshall of Baltimore City, had his soldiers arrest all adult males in the funeral party except the minister. (6)

Mixed in among those of high purpose and broken hearts were the gawkers and souvenir hunters. Fulfilling a very natural impulse to be curious, they put an additional strain on roads, food and lodging at this critical time. One of these was Mr. Henry Gore of Reisterstown. Gore visited Gettysburg immediately after the fighting was over. Walking across the battlefield he stopped to inspect the body of a dead Confederate. From the soldier's pocket he removed a Lutheran hymnal, the pages tinted red from the blood of its previous owner. (7)

Thomas E. Van Bebber, Esq., was an articulate member of Baltimore society. He took a tour of the battlefield about three weeks after the fighting had ceased, in company with a clergyman and a few ladies. Van Bebber called the battlefield a " . . . painfully attractive spot . . ." with trampled field and small tent encampments sheltering the wounded. He went on to write:

> "The state of things continued for several miles, until we came upon a region of desolation, where half-decayed carcasses of mules and horses might be seen in every direction, so that the hot summer air was completely saturated with the sickening odor of putrefaction."

Van Bebber's party finished their first day watching the gravediggers on Cemetery Hill. The next morning they went to the Theological Seminary Hospital where they passed out words of sympathy to the wounded before returning to their arduous duty as tourists. In town they encountered a detail of men sorting out a heap of military equipment salvaged from the battlefield. From them Van Bebber acquired a military button and a letter found in the pocket of a Louisiana soldier. The letter contained a small lock of hair from each of his children plaited into a wreath and fastened to the paper with a pink ribbon. The soldier's name was Richard H. Willeford.

Passing again over Cemetery Hill, the group proceeded to Culp's Hill where ". . . the ground was thickly strewn with old clothes, cartridge boxes, canteens, beef-bones and bullets." While climbing about the breastworks, Van Bebber spotted two items about 20 yards apart. One was a deck of cards and the other the remains of a New Testament. Struck by this conflict of good and evil he selected the book as his final memento of the vast battlefield. (8)

Shortly after the battle, Governor Andrew Curtain of Pennsylvania appointed David Wells his agent to purchase land on Cemetery Hill for a soldier's cemetery. By August of 1863, five lots on the west side of the Baltimore Pike were acquired. (9)

With winter not far off, it was important to remove as many bodies as possible from their temporary graves while penciled names and other fragile means of identification still existed. F.W. Biesecker was awarded the contract to transfer the bodies from the battlefield to the cemetery for the sum of $1.59 each. Items found with the bodies were used to identify the remains, if not by name, at least by the state from which they served. The contractor kept a complete inventory of the items recovered and submitted it as a separate report after the work was done. Only one Marylander was on the list. Found with David Krebs, Company G, First Potomac Home Brigade was, "25 cents, one tassel, one smoker, etc." (10)

On November 19, 1863, just five months after the battle, the Soldiers National Cemetery was dedicated. This occasion was immortalized by President Lincoln's Gettysburg Address. Of the 3555 soldiers buried there, only 22 are from the state of Maryland. No Confederate soldiers were allowed in the cemetery but some misidentification was inevitable, especially from a state with men in both armies. Among those he fought against lies Private Minon F. Knott, Company F, First Maryland Battalion C.S.A. Buried in nearby Evergreen Cemetery is Private Hiram H. Hartman, Company K, First Potomac Home Brigade, killed in action on July 3, 1863. (11)

The only Maryland command to be sent to Gettysburg after the battle was the Patapsco Guards. The Guards were an independent company of infantry organized in Ellicott Mill's in the latter part of 1861. The company was never assimilated into a regimental formation. It was stationed at York, Pennsylvania, during the Gettysburg Campaign and skirmished with Gordon's Brigade at Wrightsville prior to the battle.

Captain Thomas S. McGowan received orders to move his men to Gettysburg in October of 1863. There was still much work to be done in cleaning up the battlefield and guarding the hospitals. The company went into camp southeast of the town near what is now Hospital Road.

One of the men in the company was Hezekiah Weeks, a 21-year-old blacksmith from Howard County, Maryland. While the rest of the company pulled guard duty, Weeks was ordered to examine the hundreds of horses and mules left behind after the battle. He treated and reshod those that could be helped. The rest he shot. It was a distasteful job for a man who loved horses.

Sgt. Allen T. Fort.
Patapsco Guards. USA.

In September, Weeks and a few of his friends went to Cashtown, 11 miles west of Gettysburg, to escape the misery of the battlefield and hospital wards. Most of the men headed for the tavern, but Weeks wanted to see what he could buy in the general store. In the store was a squad of Confederate soldiers buying provisions. They were hiding out in the countryside, unable to find their way back to the Potomac River. This was eight weeks after the battle! After a friendly chat both parties went on their way. In late December, the Patapsco Guards Independent Company of Maryland Infantry returned to their post at York. (12)

Pvt. Henry Holliday's photograph of the Maryland Confederate monument on Culp's Hill. Note plaque on back reads "First Maryland" while "Second Maryland" is carved on the base in front.

Chapter 3

THE VETERANS

The transition from battlefield to National Park at Gettysburg began almost immediately after the armies marched south. One month after the battle, David McConaughy, in an unprecedented act of foresight, solicited aid from leading Gettysburg citizens to preserve the battlefield as a memorial to the soldiers who fought there. Although not personally successful, his idea was fostered by others and evolved into one of the most famous battlefield parks in the world.

At the same time McConaughy was attempting to buy land, Governor Curtin's concern for the Union dead quickly resulted in the establishment of the Soldiers National Cemetery which was incorporated in April of 1864. One commissioner was appointed from each of the 18 loyal states that participated in the battle. Mr. B. DeFord represented the state of Maryland. As early as December of 1863, a committee was formed to design a monument for the cemetery. Captain John S. Berry of Maryland served on this committee. The Soldiers National Monument was dedicated on July 1, 1869. (1)

Also in 1864 the Gettysburg Battlefield Memorial Association was chartered. It was the first agency to manage the development of the park and supervise the erection of monuments and markers on the battlefield. The first monuments were appropriately raised by the state of Pennsylvania in 1883.

THE MARYLAND CONFEDERATE MONUMENT

On August 11, 1885, the Vice President of the Gettysburg Battlefield Memorial Association read a letter to its board of directors from the veterans of the First Maryland Battalion requesting permission to erect a monument on Culp's Hill. This was the first application by a unit from the Confederate Army. The association's decision to approve the application was endorsed by the Pennsylvania Department of the Grand Army of the Republic at its annual reunion, which was being held in Gettysburg at the same time. (2)

The following April a committee from the First Maryland submitted the design for their proposed monument. Being the first "enemy" marker on the field, the Gettysburg Battlefield Memorial Association was naturally tentative in its decision process. First its location had to be arbitrated. The committee, composed of Col. W. Zollinger, Lamar Hollyday, and George Probet, chose a site within the line of Union works on Culp's Hill which the First Maryland had captured on the night of July 2. The resident committee members were not willing to set such a momentous precedent and looked to the board of directors for a final decision. On June 4, the directors issued instructions to the Maryland committee ". . . that they will be required to erect their proposed monument on this field outside the Union breastworks, facing them and the inscription of said monument to be subject to approval of this Association." (3)

The wording on the plaque had to be changed from ". . . captured the line of works . . ." to ". . . occupied the line of works . . ." Survivors of the fighting on Culp's Hill wondered how occupying a position at gun point could be any different than capturing it. Still, this was a major step in uniting the veterans.

Finally the Monument Association decreed that since there were two Maryland Union regiments on Culp's Hill, it would be too confusing to have a Confederate unit with the same number. On the base of the monument would be inscribed "First Maryland Infantry changed to Second Maryland Infantry." (4)

The monument to the First/Second Maryland Infantry was dedicated on November 19, 1886. The ceremony was attended by 2000 soldiers, citizens, and dignitaries. Veterans organizations included the Society of the Army and Navy of the Confederate States in Maryland, Murray Association, Ladies Confederate Memorial Association, and veterans of the various Maryland commands that fought for the South at Gettysburg. The Fifth Maryland Regiment of the Maryland National Guard under the command of Colonel Steuart Brown provided an escort for the occasion and Latchford's Drum Corps, composed of sons of Union veterans, the cadence.

The route of the procession was out Carlisle Street to Baltimore Street, across Cemetery Hill and then left to Culp's Hill. For those returning to the scene of the battle the landscape must have evoked both fond and tragic memories of their days as a soldier. When the attendees had gathered at the site of the dedication, a floral anchor was placed at the base of the monument by a mother whose son had served in the battalion. General George Hume Steuart presided over the ceremonies. Rev. Randolph H. McKim, the sole surviving member of his staff, led the assembly in prayer. During the dedication ceremonies the Fifth Regiment band played two dirges, but refrained from playing any music associated with either side of the recent conflict. Captain George Thomas delivered the dedication address. At its conclusion Mr. John M. Krauth accepted the monument on behalf of the Gettysburg Battlefield Memorial Association. The Maryland Battalion had made the first permanent lodgment by Confederate troops on the battlefield at Gettysburg. (5)

DESCRIPTION OF THE MARYLAND CONFEDERATE MONUMENT

The monument to the First/Second Maryland Infantry Battalion is located on Culp's Hill and faces the line of Union breastworks captured on the night of July 2, 1863. It is constructed of white granite and stands approximately 10 feet high. The shaft sits on a small base with an oversized cap that comes to a point which holds a black sphere representing a cannonball. All four sides of the cap contain a Cross Bottony or Maryland Cross, symbolic of Confederate service. The obverse side of the shaft contains the state coat of arms. On the base is inscribed:

"2nd MD. INFANTRY C.S.A."

The reverse side contains a recessed tablet with the following inscription:

"The First Maryland Battalion Infantry
Lieut. Col. Jas. R. Herbert
Stewart's Brigade
Johnson's Division
Ewell's Corps
Army of Northern Virginia
Advanced from Rock Creek
About 7 P.M. July 2nd
occupied the line of works at this point and held it's
position until next morning."

The Maryland Confederate Monument.

Ribbon worn by Theodore Lang at the
dedication of Union monuments in 1888.

THE UNION MONUMENTS

The same year the Confederate monument was dedicated, the Dushane Post #3 of the Grand Army of the Republic in Baltimore City formed a committee to introduce a bill in the State Legislature to erect monuments at Gettysburg for each of the Maryland Union regiments engaged there. Because the project relied on government funding and not private donations as the Confederate monument had, it was two years before the bill was introduced. At a meeting in the Dushane Post Hall on February 20, 1888, Colonel George W. Vernon said, "Future generations . . . would indeed feel mortified, and humiliated to visit the great battlefield of Gettysburg, the best marked field of ancient or modern times, and not see . . . a single monument to commemorate the part the sons of Maryland took in that great struggle . . . ."

A few days later Theodore F. Lang, the Department Commander of Maryland G.A.R.; Frank Nolen, the man who had first suggested the monument project; and several other Union veterans met with the Finance Committee of the State Senate to explain their proposed bill. Senator C. Ridgley Goodwin, a Confederate veteran and member of the Finance Committee, requested the honor of introducing the bill in the Senate which passed both houses unanimously and was signed by Governor E.E. Jackson on March 23, 1888. (6)

The following June a committee of two officers and one enlisted man from each of the regiments and Rigby's Battery went to Gettysburg to select the locations for their monuments. General Henry H. Lockwood accompanied them. All of the men were survivors of the battle and all the commanding officers but one were on the committee. Colonel James Wallace of the First Eastern Shore Infantry Regiment was deceased and Lt. Colonel William Comegys served in his place. (7)

Maryland Day at Gettysburg was Thursday, October 25, 1888. The Western Maryland Railroad ran five special trains for the occasion. The Cumberland Valley also ran a special from Martinsburg via Williamsport and Hagerstown. The Baltimore and Ohio Railroad established a one-rate fare from any point in the state to Baltimore or Hagerstown so that those attending the dedication could easily connect with one of the specials. (8)

It was after twelve noon before all the trains had arrived and the great parade was ready to begin. The order of march was as follows:

General Steuart Brown of the Maryland National Guard and staff

THE COMMISSION.

MARYLAND'S

TRIBUTE

TO HER LOYAL SONS!

OCTOBER 25th, 1888.

DEDICATION

OF THE

MONUMENTS

ERECTED BY

The State of Maryland,

TO COMMEMORATE

THE HEROISM OF HER TROOPS,

AT THE

BATTLE OF GETTYSBURG,

July, 1863.

1st Regt. (E. S.) Md. Vol. Infy.

1st Regt. (P.H.B.) Md. Vol. Inf.

3d Regt. Md. Vol. Infantry.

1st Regt. Maryland Cavalry.

Rigby's Batt'y A, 1st Md. Lt. A.

DCT

Dedication ribbon, 1888.

FIRST DIVISION

The Fifth Regiment Band and Drum Corps
Fifth Regiment M.N.G., Lt. Col. Boykin commanding
Color Sgt. J.S. Bull carrying Governor's Flag
Carriages containing Governor Jackson, the Mayor of Baltimore,
    and the Monument Commission
Baltimore Light Infantry Band and Drum Corps
Baltimore Light Infantry, Lt. Col. Barry commanding

SECOND DIVISION

Col. T.F. Lang, Department Commander G.A.R.
Wilson Post Drum Corps, 20 pieces
Wilson Post #1 G.A.R. (Baltimore), 75 men
Reynolds Post #2 G.A.R. (Frederick), 10 men
Dushane Post Drum Corps, 20 pieces
Dushane Post #3 G.A.R. (Baltimore), 125 men
Dushane Post Guard, 20 men
Reno Post #4 G.A.R. (Hagerstown), 15 men
Tyler Post #5 G.A.R. (Cumberland), 12 men
Custer Post #6 G.A.R. (Baltimore), 20 men
Latchford Camp, Sons of Veterans Drum Corps
Denison Post #8 G.A.R. (Woodberry), 35 men
Wingate Post #9 G.A.R. (Annapolis), 10 men
Burns' Post Drum Corps
Burns' Post #13 G.A.R. (Westminster), 35 men
Antietam Post #14 G.A.R. (Sharpsburg), 10 men
Guy Post Drum Corps
Guy Post #16 G.A.R. (Baltimore), 25 men
Lincoln Post #7 G.A.R. (Baltimore), 25 men
Beattie Post #15 G.A.R. (Street), 10 men
Burnside Post #22 G.A.R. (Baltimore), 30 men
Hick's Post #24 G.A.R. (Easton), 27 men
Gosnell Post #39 G.A.R. (Glyndon), 10 men
T. Stevens' Post #40 G.A.R. (New Windsor), 10 men
Arthur Post #41 G.A.R. (Emmitsburg), 15 men
Middletown Cornet Band
A.C. Spicer Post #43 G.A.R. (Eklo), 25 men
Ellsworth Camp Sons of Veterans, 25 men
Survivors Purnell Legion, 25 men
Surviors Third Maryland, 30 men
Survivors Rigby's Battery, 11 men

Survivors First Eastern Shore and First Potomac Home Brigade and others, 100 men
American Band and Drum Corps
Veteran Volunteer Firemen, 100 men
Ladies Relief Corps of the Denison Post, 40 members

The column conducted by Major Charles A. Hale, Battlefield Guide, marched from Baltimore Street to the Soldiers National Cemetery, around the monument and then to Culp's Hill where it passed along the line of breastworks contested by the Maryland regiments. Many of the men marching in the ranks of the Maryland National Guard on this day had been mortal enemies here in 1863.

At Spangler's Spring a temporary stand had been erected for the day's speakers. Reverend Samuel Kramer, formerly the Chaplain of the Third Maryland Regiment, offered a prayer. Then Colonel Lang introduced a speaker from each of the five Maryland commands whose monuments were being dedicated. This was followed by a brief oration by Colonel James Mullikin, a survivor of the First Eastern Shore Regiment. Then Colonel Lang presented the monuments to Governor Jackson who, in turn, delivered them to the care of the Gettysburg Battlefield Memorial Association. John M. Krauth accepted the monuments on behalf of the association. Reverend Kramer closed the proceedings with a benediction. (9)

DESCRIPTION OF THE MONUMENTS

The cost for each monument was $900. The five sites they were placed on were purchased for a total of $1000.

FIRST EASTERN SHORE INFANTRY REGIMENT

All three infantry regiment monuments are located on Culp's Hill where they were engaged on July 2 and 3, 1863. The First Eastern Shore monument contains a life size figure of a soldier in alto relief lying behind breastworks with cocked musket. The block on which the relief is carved is 7 feet long and 4.5 feet tall.

The obverse side contains the coat of arms of the state in bronze surrounded by the inscription:

1ST REG'T EASTERN SHORE
MARYLAND VOL. INFANTRY.
COL. JAS. WALLACE.
LOCKWOOD'S INDEPENDENT BRIG.
12TH CORPS.

MARYLAND'S TRIBUTE TO HER LOYAL SONS.

"Five companies held the works in front of this stone on the morning of July 3d, 1863, relieving other troops and remaining until about noon when they were relieved. The remainder of the regiment were in position during the same time about three hundred yards to the right.

Organized at Cambridge, Md., Sept., 1861. Consolidated with the 11th Md. Inf'y, Feb. 25th, 1865. Effective strength July 3d, 1863, 583. Casualties: Killed 5. Wounded 18. Missing 2. Total 25."

The reverse side contains the Twelfth Corps Star and:

"1st Reg't Eastern Shore
Maryland Vol. Infantry,
Col. Jas. Wallace,
Lockwood's Independent Brig.
12th Corps.
Maryland's Tribute to her Loyal Sons."

FIRST REGIMENT POTOMAC HOME BRIGADE INFANTRY

The base is carved from granite taken from the battlefield and measures four and one-half feet square. The die is polished and contains the state seal and history of the regiment. The cap is made up of four rolled blankets topped off with a five point star representing the badge of the Twelfth Corps. On the star are carved a belt with cartridge box and sheathed bayonet. The total height of the monument is 13 feet. The inscriptions read as follows:

FRONT:

"1st Maryland
Regiment
Potomac Home
Brigade,
Vol. Infantry,
Col. Wm. P. Maulsby,
Lockwood's Independent
Brigade.
12th Corps.
Maryland's Tribute to her Loyal Sons"

3d
MARYLAND INF'TY

Col. Joseph M. Sudsburg

1st BRIG. 1st DIV. 12th CORPS

JULY 2nd 1863.
OCCUPIED THIS POSITION IN RESERVE.
LATE IN THE AFTERNOON MOVED
TO REINFORCE THE LEFT OF THE LINE,
RETURNING ABOUT 8 P. M.
AND FINDING THE WORKS OCCUPIED
BY THE ENEMY.

MARYLAND'S TRIBUTE TO HER LOYAL SONS.

RIGHT:

>"July 2d, Reinforced the Left Wing between 5 and 6
>O'clock p.m. charging under the immediate direction of
>Gen. Meade and re-capturing three pieces of artillery
>
>July 3rd, Engaged the enemy at this point from 5 to 6
>O'clock a.m. At 11 a.m. went to the assistance of the 2d
>Div. 12th Corps, engaging the enemy there for about
>four hours."

LEFT:

>"Effective strength 739. Casualties: Killed 23. Wounded
>80. Missing 1. Total 104.
>Organized at Frederick, Md., from Aug. 15th to Dec.
>13th, 1861.

>**PRINCIPAL ENGAGEMENTS**
>Maryland Heights, Md, Sept. 13th, 1862.
>Gettysburg, Pa. July 2d-3d, 1863.
>Monocacy, Md., July 9th. 1864.
>and eight skirmishes.
>Mustered out May 29th, 1865."

THIRD MARYLAND REGIMENT VETERAN VOLUNTEERS

This monument is similar to that of the First Potomac Home Brigade. The shaft is of New Hampshire granite 13 feet high on a secondary base 3 feet 10 inches high and 2 feet 2 inches square. The front and back of the base are polished tablets. On the front are crossed muskets supporting a cartridge box over the state seal. The sides and back hold raised tablets in rough pointed work. The cap is 2 feet 10 inches square with a Twelfth Corps star on all four sides.

FRONT:

>"3d
>Maryland Infty.
>Col. Joseph M. Sudsburg
>1st Brig. 1st Div. 12 Corps
>
>July 2d, 1863,
>Occupied this position in reserve. Late in the afternoon

MARYLAND'S TRIBUTE TO HER LOYAL SONS

POSITION OF THE
1ST. REGT. MD. CAV.
LT. COL. JAMES M. DEEMS.
1ST. BRIG. 2ND. DIV. CAVALRY CORPS.
IN THE CAVALRY ENGAGEMENT ON THIS FLANK.
JULY 3D. 1863.

moved to re-inforce the left of the line. Returning about 9 p.m. and finding the works occupied by the enemy.

Maryland's Tribute to Her Loyal Sons."

RIGHT:

"July 3d.
Under fire in reserve until about noon, then occupied the works in front and held them until relieved. Losing in killed Capt. Henry Fenton, Co. G, Wounded, 1 Officer and 6 men."

LEFT:

"PRINCIPAL ENGAGEMENTS.

Cedar Mountain, Va.,	Aug. 9, 1862.
Chantilly, Va.,	Sept. 1, "
Antietam, Md.,	Sept, 17, "
Chancellorsville, Va.,	May 1,2,3, 1863.
Gettysburg, Pa.,	July 2,3, "
Wilderness, Va.,	May 5,6,7, 1864.
Spotsylvania, Va.,	May 10,11,12, "
Cold Harbor., Va,	June 5-12, "
Petersburg, Va., (Charge)	June 17, "
Petersburg, Va., (Siege)	1864-1865.
Petersburg, Va., (Crater)	July 31, 1864.
Petersburg, Va., (Assault and Capture)	April 2,3, 1865."

REAR:

"Organized at Baltimore, Md., May 11, 1862.
Re-enlisted Feb. 4, 1864.
Mustered out July 31, 1865."

FIRST REGIMENT MARYLAND VOLUNTEER CAVALRY

This monument is located on the East Cavalry Battlefield. It stands 10 feet 4 inches tall on a 6 foot 4 inch square base and is made of Hardwick granite. The cap contains a horseshoe in bas-relief with a horse's head in the center and crossed swords underneath. On the front is the bronze medallion coat of arms and the inscription:

"Maryland's Tribute to Her Loyal Sons
Position of the 1st Regt. Md. Cav.
Lt. Col. James M. Deems,
1st Brig. 2nd Div. Cavalry Corps,
in the Cavalry Engagement on this
flank, July 3d, 1863."

REVERSE:

"Organized at Baltimore, Md.,
November, 1861. Participated
in sixty-two engagements including
the following:

Charlestown, Va.,	May 28, 1862.
2d Bull Run,	Aug. 29,30, "
Stoneman's Raid, Va.,	Apr. and May, 1863.
Brandy Station, Va.,	June 9, "
Aldie, Va.,	" 19, "
Gettysburg, Pa.,	July 2-3, "
Deep Bottom, Va.,	Aug. 16-18, 1864.
Five Forks, Va.,	Apr. 4, 1865.
Appomattox Court House, Va.,	" "

Casualties in action
during the War.

	Officers	Men	Total
Killed	1	32	33
Wounded	10	147	157
Captured or Missing	12	208	220
Aggregate			410

Mustered out Aug. 8, 1865."

RIGBY'S BATTERY "A" FIRST MARYLAND LIGHT ARTILLERY

Built of Hardwick granite, the base is 5 feet 4 inches square and the monument stands 11 feet 6 inches high. It sits upon a rock on the summit of Powers Hill. Next to the monument is a three inch Rodman gun. Carved on the front are two crossed cannons. Wrapped around the cannons is the inscription "Rigby's Maryland Battery A." A polished ball 2 feet in diameter is set on the point cap of the shaft. The face of the die is polished and bears the bronze coat of arms and the inscription "Maryland's Tribute to Her Loyal Sons."

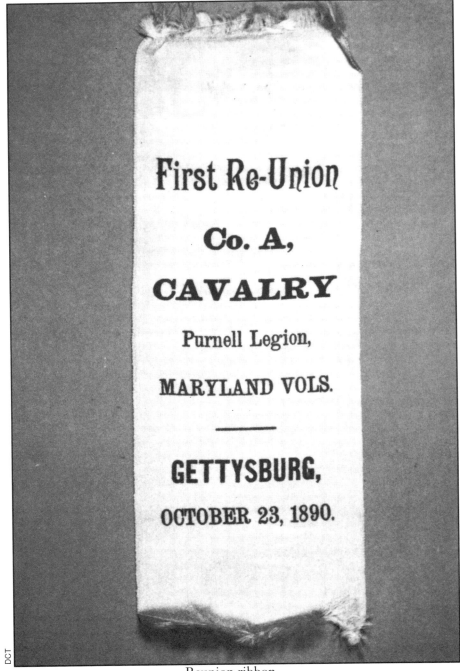

Reunion ribbon.

REAR:

"PRINCIPAL ENGAGEMENTS.

Seven days battle before Richmond, Va., 1862.
Crampton's Gap, Md.,   Sep 14,   "
Antietam, Md.,   " 17,   "
Fredericksburg, Va.,   Dec. 13,   "
2nd Fredericksburg,   May 3-4, 1863.
Gettysburg, Pa.,   July 2-3, 1863.

Rigby's Battery "A" 1st Maryland Artillery,
Capt. Jas. H. Rigby occupied this position on the morning of July 2d, 1863, and remained in Battery until the termination of the Battle; engaging a battery of the enemy on the 2nd, and the morning of the 3rd. shelling the woods in front for nearly three hours, assisting in driving out the enemy."

RIGHT:

"Organized at Baltimore, Md.,
October, 1861. Consolidated with
Battery "B" Maryland Light Artillery,
March 11, 1865."

LEFT:

"Losses in action (During the war)
Killed 5. Wounded 18.
Missing 3. Total 26.
Strength at Gettysburg.
Officers 4. Enlisted men 102."

COMPANY A, PURNELL LEGION CAVALRY

When the Gettysburg Monument Commission issued its final report, it recommended that three additional monuments be placed on the battlefield: One on Culp's Hill where the companies of the First Eastern Shore Regiment fought under Colonel Wallace, one on the Union left where the First Potomac Home Brigade re-captured three pieces of artillery from Longstreet's men, and one on the East Cavalry Battlefield where the Purnell Legion Company fought on July 3. Only the last recommendation was acted on.

Dedication of the Purnell Legion monument took place on October 23, 1890. The day was cold and rainy, but a group of 150 persons braved the elements to attend the ceremonies. Colonel William H. Love repre-

sented the Governor of Maryland. Also in attendance was Doctor George R. Graham, the Department Commander of Maryland for the G.A.R., and a number of surviving members of the Purnell Legion.

The dedication was held at the monument located on the Rummell Farm near the First Maryland Cavalry monument. Captain William Gibson gave an address in which he sketched the history of the Purnell Legion. Immediately after the exercise the first reunion of Company A was held at the City Hotel in Gettysburg. (10)

THE PURNELL LEGION MONUMENT

The front of the monument represents a dismounted cavalryman with carbine and complete accouterments. The life size figure is done in alto relief. Beneath the kneeling figure is inscribed:

"Co. A, Purnell Legion.
Maryland Cavalry.
Maryland's Tribute to her Loyal Sons."

RIGHT:

"1st Brigade."

LEFT:

"2nd Division."

REAR:

"This detached Company,
Commanded by Capt. Robert E. Duvall.
Served in the Cavalry Engagement
On the flank, July 2nd and 3rd, 1863.
Organized at Pikesville, Md., Sept., Oct., and Nov., 1861.
Mustered out at Fort Monroe, Va., July 28, 1865.
(Cavalry Corps Badge)
Cavalry Corps."

Governor E. E. Jackson and staff at the dedication of Maryland Monuments, Gettysburg, October 25, 1888.

THE 50th ANNIVERSARY REUNION

As the years passed the veterans from both armies often returned to Gettysburg singularly or in groups for special ceremonies. State by state, monuments, plaques and memorials continued to populate the fields that had once held so much terror and death. After the turn of the century, the automobile made Gettysburg the ideal destination for day trips and

Veteran's medal from 50th reunion.

weekend excursions. With the same foresight it had in 1863, the state of Pennsylvania proposed a grand reunion of the Blue and Gray. A special commission was formed in 1909 with representatives from all the states, territories, and the Federal Government to plan for a 50th Anniversary Reunion. Senator Isidor Rayner represented the state of Maryland on this commission.

The joint reunion of the Grand Army of the Republic and the United Confederate Veterans took place on July 1-4, 1913. Some 54,000 veterans averaging over 70 years of age came to the town that had been made famous by war—their war. All had not participated in the battle, but each man knew the impact it had on American history.

Maryland veterans received a 50th Anniversary Reunion medal. The top bar was inscribed MARYLAND. From it hung a triangular medal connected by a black and gold ribbon, the state colors. Inside the triangle was a full color state coat of arms. (11)

Before the reunion ended, Governor John K. Tener of Pennsylvania issued an invitation to the veterans to return to Gettysburg in 1938 on the 75th anniversary of the battle for a final joint reunion of the Blue and Gray.

Civil War Army Nurses at Gettysburg.
50th Anniversary Reunion.

THE 75th ANNIVERSARY REUNION

Governor George H. Earl kept the promise made by his predecessor. In 1935 he issued a formal invitation to the United Confederate Veterans and the Grand Army of the Republic at their respective national meetings. A joint committee from the state of Pennsylvania and the Federal Government arranged all aspects of transportation, housing, and the ceremonies to be held between June 29 and July 6, 1938. (12)

It is remarkable to note that at an average age of 90 years old, 1845 veterans attended the last joint reunion. Of these, 1359 were Union and 486 Confederate. Each veteran was given a wall tent for himself and a personal attendant. Of the 22 veterans that gave their residence as Maryland, only one wore Confederate gray, Private E. Scott Dance, of the First Maryland Cavalry. (13)

On Saturday July 2, a Reunion Parade was held. Representing the state of Maryland were the Campaign Post No. 195 of the V.F.W. Drum and Bugle Corps and the American Legion Drum and Bugle Corps, both from Baltimore City, and the Morris Frock Post No. 42 American Legion Junior Drum and Bugle Corps from Hagerstown.

Last reunion of the Blue and Gray at Gettysburg, 1938.

Veteran's pin from 75th reunion, 1938.

On Sunday, Father William F. Culhane retraced the steps of Father Burlando from Emmitsburg 75 years earlier. He delivered a sermon during the Army Field Mass. That afternoon a crowd of nearly half a million people gathered to see President Franklin D. Roosevelt dedicate the Eternal Light Peace Memorial located on Oak Hill. It was the largest event in the history of Gettysburg. (14)

As the last reunion of the Blue and the Gray came to a conclusion, their earthly presence was nearly at an end. One veteran died on the last day of the reunion. Another six did not survive the trip home. All were marching toward their final muster. Soon Gettysburg would be without its veterans, but it would never be without their memories and their monuments. (15)

Pocket size, turn-of-the-century guidebook.

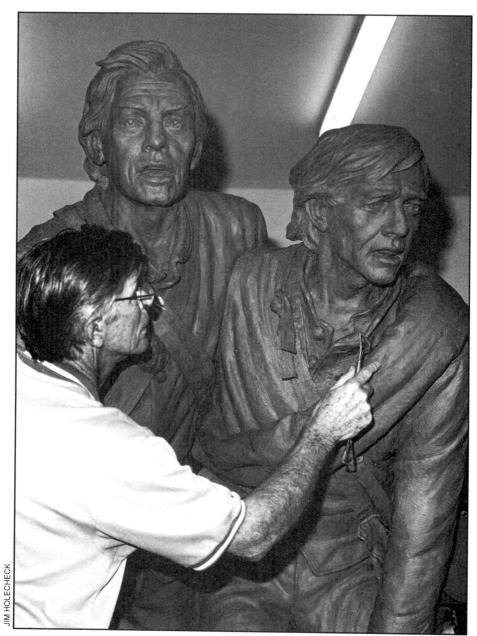

Mr. Ludtke at work on the clay model before casting.

Chapter 4

THE FINAL TRIBUTE

The Gettysburg National Military Park has become an international landmark for the American Civil War. Every year over one million people visit the park. Many go to retrace the steps of relatives or personal heroes who participated in the great battle. In 1989 a man by the name of James Holechek went to the park with a greater ambition. He was looking for the heritage of his state and was disappointed to learn that of the over 1300 monuments, markers, and memorials at the park, none of them officially represented the state of Maryland which, because of its divided loyalties, made the state's participation in the battle unlike any other.

The following year Mr. Holechek, a retired advertising executive from Baltimore, founded Citizens for a Maryland Monument at Gettysburg—a non-profit organization with a board of trustees composed of 20 members drawn from the business, government, and educational communities in the state. The Honorable William Donald Schaefer, Governor of Maryland, was the Honorary Chairman and actively supported the project from start to finish.

For the next three years Jim Holechek canvassed the state soliciting contributions and gaining the support of reenactors, historical societies, and the Baltimore Civil War Round Table. In 1990 he and Trustee Courtney B. Wilson appeared before the state legislature and secured a matching grant of $75,000. At the same time, the monument commission opened a national competition for qualified sculptors. The renowned Baltimore sculptor, Reuben Kramer, agreed to chair the judging committee. Three semifinalists were selected from a field of 83. Each submitted an 18-inch high clay model for the final judging. The winner was Mr. Lawrence M. Ludtke of Houston, Texas. Mr. Ludtke was awarded a $75,000 contract to sculpt the two figures. Each of the runners-up received $1500 for their efforts.

As public awareness grew so did support for the monument. Governor Schaefer personally donated $1000 to the project and encouraged many others to do the same. Citizens throughout the state pitched in to help in any way they could. In the fall of 1993 members of the Flower Basket Committee from the Talbot County Women's Club planted 3000 daffodils and tulips at the monument site in red, white, black and gold to represent the colors of the state flag.

Mr. Holechek also secured the volunteer services of J. Vinton Schafer and Sons of White Marsh to manage construction at the monument site and the firm of Frederick Ward and Associates of Bel Air to design and engineer the viewing plaza.

During the months he worked on the project, Mr. Ludtke hung a Maryland State flag outside his studio and played the sound track from the movie "Gettysburg" for inspiration. He commemorated the 131st anniversary of the Battle of Gettysburg by completing the larger than life clay figures on July 1, 1994.

The actual construction of the monument was performed at Shidoni Foundry in Tesuque, New Mexico. When completed, the bronze soldiers stood nine feet high and weighed in at 2000 pounds.

By the time the statue was mounted on its pedestal and the plaza completed, over $200,000 was expended on the project including a $10,000 endowment required by the Park Service for perpetual care of the monument. Add to this figure the value of services rendered in promotion, construction, transportation and landscaping—all donated by the citizens of Maryland—and the actual cost of the monument could have easily reached $300,000 and may never have been built. It is interesting to note that the total cost for all five Union monuments erected in 1888 was $5500 and the one Confederate monument in 1886 cost $1000.

THE DEDICATION

Sunday, November 13, 1994, was again Maryland Day at Gettysburg. One hundred and thirty-one years after the battle both sides were reunited in the only state memorial dedicated to service in both armies. The official starting time for the program was 1 p.m. with music provided by the Maryland National Guard band. A small army of Civil War reenactors in authentic uniforms marched to the state song "Maryland My Maryland." Official representatives from the state and federal government and the Gettysburg National Military Park added dignity and purpose to this historic event.

Above the wreath laying and excellent speeches there was an overwhelming sense of state pride. The combination of artistic design and the meticulous attention to detail by the implementation committee and the governor's staff made the event in many ways a re-creation of the ceremonies held on Culp's Hill on November 19, 1886, when the first Maryland monument was dedicated at Gettysburg. The veterans would have approved.

DESCRIPTION OF THE MARYLAND MEMORIAL

Located at the southwest corner of the Cyclorama parking lot near the Taneytown Road, the site combines a view of Culp's Hill where the majority of Marylanders fought during the battle and easy access to the Cyclorama and Gettysburg Visitors Center.

Two nine-foot bronze soldiers, one Union and one Confederate both wounded, support each other in the aftermath of the great battle. The figures stand atop a four-and-a-half foot pedestal of granite. On the obverse is carved the word "MARYLAND" in 10-inch letters. In the center is a bronze state seal cast from the medallion on the Rigby's Battery monument which stands on nearby Powers Hill. One side of the monument contains the checkered heraldry of Lord Calvert. The other the Bottony or "Maryland" cross. On the reverse is mounted a bronze tablet with the inscription on the following page:

A FINAL TRIBUTE

MORE THAN 3,000 MARYLANDERS SERVED ON BOTH SIDES OF THE CONFLICT AT THE BATTLE OF GETTYSBURG. THEY COULD BE FOUND IN ALL BRANCHES OF THE ARMY FROM THE RANK OF PRIVATE TO MAJOR GENERAL AND ON ALL PARTS OF THE BATTLEFIELD. BROTHER AGAINST BROTHER WOULD BE THEIR LEGACY, PARTICULARLY ON THE SLOPES OF CULP'S HILL. THIS MEMORIAL SYMBOLIZES THE AFTERMATH OF THAT BATTLE AND THE WAR. BROTHERS AGAIN. MARYLANDERS ALL.

THE STATE OF MARYLAND PROUDLY HONORS IT SONS WHO FOUGHT AT GETTYSBURG IN DEFENSE OF THE CAUSES THEY HELD SO DEAR.

PARTICIPATING MARYLAND COMMANDS

UNION

1ST EASTERN SHORE INFANTRY
1ST POTOMAC HOME BRIGADE INFANTRY
3RD INFANTRY
1ST CAVALRY
CO. A PURNELL LEGION CAVALRY
BATTERY A, 1ST ARTILLERY

CONFEDERATE

2ND INFANTRY
1ST CAVALRY
1ST ARTILLERY
2ND ARTILLERY (BALTIMORE LIGHT)
4TH ARTILLERY (CHESAPEAKE)

NOTES

CHAPTER 1

1. *Richard S. Andrews, A Memoir, Edited by Tunstall Smith*, (Baltimore 1910), p. 15; *Official Records of the Union and Confederate Armies*, 128 Volumes, (Washington, D.C.: Government Printing Office 1880-1901) Series I, Vol. 27, Part I, pp. 155-168, Part II, pp. 283-291; hereafter referenced as OR's.
2. Frank M. Myers, *The Comanches: A History of White's Battalion, Virginia Cavalry*. (Baltimore: 1871), pp. 7-8, 18.
3. Robert K. Krick, *Lee's Colonels*, (Dayton, OH: 1979), p. 366.
4. Meyers, pp. 192-193; Champ Clark, *Gettysburg: The Confederate High Tide*, (Alexandria, VA: 1985), p. 30.
5. *History and Roster of Maryland Volunteers, War of 1861-5*. Volume I; hereafter referenced as Roster. L. Allison Willmer et al, (Baltimore: 1898) Vol. I, p. 782.
6. Harry W. Pfanz, *Gettysburg: Culp's Hill & Cemetery Hill*, (Chapel Hill: 1993), p. 162; OR's Vol. 27, Part I, p. 238; Part III, p. 262.
7. Clark, p. 33.
8. Ezra J. Warner, *Generals in Gray*, (LSU: 1959), p. 11. George T. Ness, *The Regular Army on the Eve of the Civil War*, (Baltimore: 1990), p. 122.
9. Warner, p. 11; Chark, pp. 45-48; Frederick Tilberg, *Gettysburg National Military Park*, (Washington, DC: 1954), pp. 7,8.
10. Meyers, p. 198.
11. Tilberg, pp. 7-11.
12. W.W. Goldsborough, *The Maryland Line in the Confederate Army*, (Baltimore, 1990), pp. 165-166.
13. Goldsborough, pp. 177-178.
14. Henry Kyd Douglas, *I Rode With Stonewall*, (Chapel Hill: 1940), p. 247.
15. OR's, Vol. 27, Part II, p. 286.
16. Goldsborough, p. 11.
17. Goldsborough, p. 65.
18. Goldsborough, p. 18.
19. Pfanz, p. 154.

20. *Report of the Maryland Monument Commission*, (Baltimore: 1891), pp. 103-105; hereafter referenced as MMC.
21. Roster, pg. 483.
22. OR's, Vol. 27, Part III, p. 267.
23. OR's, Vol. 27, Part III, p. 165.
24. MMC, pp. 56-58. OR's, Vol. 27, Part I, p. 804.
25. Roster, p. 110-111.
26. OR's, Vol. 27, Part I, p. 789.
27. OR's, Vol. 27, Part I, p. 796.
28. OR's, Vol. 27, Part I, p. 795.
29. Roster, p. 142.
30. Roster, p. 797; Or's, Vol. 27, Part I, p. 168.
31. Pfanz, p. 291.
32. OR's, Vol. 27, Part I, p. 899; MMC, p. 35.
33. OR's, Series 3, Vol. I, pp. 463, 476.
34. OR's, Series E, Vol. I, p. 512.
35. OR's, Vol. 25, Part II, p. 591; Vol. 27, Part II, pp. 496-497.
36. OR's, Vol. 25, Part II, p. 591; Vol. 27, Part II, pp. 496-497.
37. OR's, Vol. 27, Part III, p. 327; Col. James Wallace, Our March to Gettysburg, published in *Our Country*, Ed. by Mrs. Lincoln Phelps, (Baltimore: 1864), pp. 3-14.
38. Pfantz, p. 180.
39. Andrews, p. 48; Pfantz, p. 168.
40. Andrews, p. 118.
41. S.Z. Ammen, *Maryland Troops in the Confederate Army*, (Baltimore: 1879). Articles compiled from "The Telegram" pp. 131-132; Pfantz, p. 179.
42. Pfantz, pp. 170-171, 183-184; OR's, Vol. 27, Part I, p. 168.
43. Goldsborough, pp. 259, 264.
44. Ammen, p. 186.
45. Pfantz, p. 181.
46. Pfantz, pp. 184, 185; Goldsborough, p. 324.
47. Ammen, p. 182; Goldsborough, p. 325.
48. Andrews, pp. 49, 120-122; Pjantz, pp. 187-188; Goldsborough, pp. 324, 325.
49. Ammen, p. 182.
50. Pfantz, p. 217.
51. Randolph H. McKim, *A Soldier's Recollections*, (New York: 1910), p. 196.
52. Goldsborough, pp. 104-105.
53. Ezra J. Warner, Generals In Blue, (L : 1964), p. 73; Ness, p. 250; Pfantz, pp. 272-273.

54. Goldsborough, p. 106; McKim, p. 201; Pfantz, p. 291.
55. Goldsborough, p. 106.
56. Jack Kelbaugh, "Gettysburg Remembered" Anne Arundel County History Notes, Vol. XXIV No. 4, (Linthicum: 1993) p.8.
57. Pfantz, p. 315-316.
58. Kelbaugh, p. 8.
59. Ammen, pp. 137-139; Pfanta, pp. 317-320.
60. MMC, pp. 57-58; First P.H.B. Regimental File, Toomey Archives.
61. J.A. Steiner, diary; Regimental File, Toomey Archives.
62. MMC, pp. 57-58.
63. MMC. p. 5.
64. MMC, pp. 93-94.
65. Dickson Preston, When Talbot Boys Died Fighting Each Other, "Star Democrat," (Easton: 1974).
66. Pfantz, pp. 317-320.
67. McKim, p. 207.
68. Douglas, pp. 249-253, 260.
69. Douglas, pp. 252-254.
70. Goldsborough, pp. 250-253.
71. Goldsborough, pp. 283-285.
72. MMC, pp. 164-165; Stephen Z. Starr, *The Union Cavalry in the Civil War*, (Baton Rouge: 1979), Vol. I, pp. 433-434.
73. MMC, pp. 104-105.
74. OR's Vol 27, Part I, pp. 959, 1051.
75. Clark, pp. 133-135.
76. Warner, *Generals in Gray*, pp. 11-12.
77. *Confederate Military History*, edited by Gen. Clement A. Evans, (Atlanta; 1899), Vol. II, Maryland, Gen. Bradley Johnson, pp. 159-160; Warner, *Generals in Gray*, p. 310.
78. George E. Stewart, *Pickets Charge*, (Boston: 1959), pp. 107-108; Pfantz, p. 81.
79. Stewart, pp. 178, 238-239.
80. Warner, *Generals in Gray*, p. 311.

CHAPTER 2

1. John W. Schildt, *Roads to Gettysburg*, (Parson, WV: 1978), pp. 49-50.
2. Virginia W. Beauchamp, "The Sisters and the Soldiers," *Maryland Historical Magazine*, Vol. 81, No. 2, pp. 128-133.

3. United States Christian Commission, second Report of the Committee of Maryland, (Baltimore: 1863), pp. 17-20; hereafter referenced as USCC.
4. USCC, pp. 90-92.
5. USCC, pp. 36-37.
6. Kelbaugh, Vol. XXIV, No. 5, pp. 11-12; Marold R. Manakee, *Maryland in the Civil War*, (Baltimore: 1959), p. 58.
7. Maryland National Guard Military Historical Society—Union Room Collection.
8. Thomas E. Van Bebber, "The Four Relics," *Our Country*, (Baltimore, 1864), pp. 265-270, 279-282.
9. *Soldiers' National Cemetery—Gettysburg*, Thomas Publications reprint (Gettysburg: 1988) p. 7. hereafter referenced as Soldiers'.
10. Soldiers', p. 7.
11. Soldiers', pp. 129, 133.
12. Daniel C. Toomey, *The Potapsco Guards* . . . (Baltimore: 1993), pp. 11-12; Company File, Toomey Archives.

CHAPTER 3

1. Soldiers', pp. 11, 18.
2. Jack McLaughlin, *The Long Encampment*, (New York: 1963), p. 205; Gettysburg Battlefield Memorial Association, Minutes of August 11, 1885, meeting p. 129; hereafter referenced as GBMA.
3. GBMA, June 4, 1864, p. 135.
4. McLaughlin, p. 123.
5. *Southern Historical Society Papers*, Kraus Reprint, (Millwood, NY: 1978), Vol. XIV, pp. 436-439.
6. MMC, pp. 4,6,7,21.
7. MMC, pp. 24-25.
8. MMC, pp. 38-39.
9. MMC, pp. 41-48, 76-79.
10. MMC, pp. 99-101, 115.
11. McLaughlin, p. 211.
12. Pennsylvania Commission, *Fiftieth Anniversary of the Battle of Gettysburg*, (Harrisburg: 1913), p. 10; hereafter referenced as PA Commission.
13. PA Commission, pp. 32, 33, 36, 62, 63.
14. PA Commission, pp. 106-109.
15. PA Commission, p. 37.

Appendix A

List of Casualties in the First Maryland Infantry Battalion

Taken from Goldsborough's "The Maryland Line in the Confederate Army"

Name	Rank	Co.	Remarks
Abbott, James	Private	G	wounded
Adkins, S. E.	Private	G	wounded
Alvey, James P.	Private	B	wounded
Anderson, Leroy	Private	F	wounded
Anderson, Samuel	Private	C	wounded
Barber, Joseph W.	2nd Lt.	C	wounded
Barry, Michael	Private	E	wounded
Barry, Philip	Private	A	wounded
Blackistone, William J.	1st Sgt.	A	wounded
Bolling, Thomas B.	Private	A	wounded
Bolling, Wallace	Private	A	wounded
Bond, John	Private	A	wounded
Bowley, William H.	Private	A	wounded
Boyles, Daniel	Private	G	wounded
Braddock, Charles S.	Private	A	wounded
Brandt, Alexander	Private	E	wounded
Breslin, E. W.	Private	G	wounded
Briddell, J. Edward	Cpl.	G	wounded
Broadfoot, William J.	1st Lt.	E	wounded
Brown, James A.	Private	D	killed
Brown, John	Private	E	wounded
Bruce, William	Private	A	killed
Burke, Michael	Private	E	captured
Byus, Charles E.	Private	E	wounded
Cain, John	Cpl.	E	wounded
Carey, James E.	Private	A	wounded
Cator, W. B.	Private	G	killed
Chandler, William S. J.	Private	A	wounded
Chunn, John H.	Private	B	wounded
Clagett, George H.	Private	F	wounded
Clagett, J. W.	Private	F	wounded
Clarke, Charles A.	Private	G	wounded
Clayville, Moses	Private	A	wounded
Clough, Robert H.	Private	C	wounded
Combs, Edgar	Private	B	wounded
Cushing, Robert H.	1st Sgt.	C	killed
Davis, Jacob N.	Private	A	wounded
Davis, James A.	1st Lt.	G	wounded
Davis, Michael	Private	C	killed
Dawson, Robert M.	Private	C	captured

Delozier, Thomas J.	Private	B	wounded
Dement, Benjamin F.	Private	F	wounded
Doyle, Philip	Private	F	wounded
Dulaney, Jeremiah	Private	C	killed
Dunnington, Lemuel	Private	F	wounded
Duvall, Daniel	Private	C	killed
Duvall, Tobias	Private	C	wounded
Edelin, William J.	Private	A	wounded
Edgar, Thomas	Private	C	wounded
Emory, Albert	Private	A	captured
Fallis, Edward	Private	E	wounded
Fallon, James	Private	E	wounded
Fentswait, J. R.	Private	G	wounded
Fenwick, Albert	Private	B	wounded
Ford, Henry	Private	B	wounded
Fountain, W. B.	Private	G	wounded
Freeman, Bernard	Private	A	wounded
Freeman, Francis Z.	Sgt.	B	wounded
Freeman, Thomas S.	Sgt.	B	killed
Fulton, Alexander	Private	A	wounded
Gardiner, William F.	Private	A	wounded
Glenn, Samuel T.	Private	A	wounded
Goldsborough, W. W.	Major	Staff	wounded
Gossom, J. H.	Private	G	killed
Green, Lewis	Private	D	wounded
Gwynn, Andrew J.	Captain	F	wounded
Halbig, J. S.	Private	E	wounded
Hamilton, Beale D.	Cpl.	C	wounded
Hamilton, Samuel H.	Private	C	wounded
Hammond, Charles	Private	C	wounded
Hammond, Edgar	Private	C	wounded
Hanson, Notley	Private	A	wounded
Hardesty, John W.	Private	A	killed
Hayden, George	Cpl.	B	wounded
Hayden, John A.	Private	B	wounded
Hays, John	Private	D	wounded
Herbert, James R.	Lt. Col.	Staff	wounded
Hines, Thomas J.	Private	D	wounded
Hodges, Benjamin	Private	F	wounded
Hogarthy, William	Private	D	captured
Holden, Robert	Private	F	wounded
Hollyday, Lamar	Private	A	wounded
Hopkins, Samuel J.	Private	A	wounded
Howard, D. Ridgely	Private	A	wounded
Hubball, Bernard	Private	A	captured
Hyland, John G.	2nd Lt.	F	wounded
Iglehart, James, Jr.	Private	A	killed
Ives, Leonard W.	Private	A	wounded
Jenkins, William	Sgt.	D	wounded
Keech, James H.	Private	B	wounded

Keepers, Alexis V.	Private	F	wounded
Kennedy, Arthur	Private	A	killed
Kenney, Bernard	Private	C	killed
Kerns, Cornelius	Private	D	killed
Killman, Richard G.	Private	D	wounded
Klemkiewiez, T. A.	Private	A	wounded
Knott, Minion F.	Private	F	wounded
Laird, William H.	Private	A	wounded
Lake, Craig	Private	A	wounded
Lamb, John	Private	D	captured
Lanham, Benjamin L.	Private	C	killed
Lawson, James A.	Cpl.	C	wounded
Lemates, James	Private	E	wounded
Lipscomb, Philip	Private	D	wounded
Littleford, J. S.	Private	G	killed
Lloyd, C. T.	Private	A	killed
Loane, W. T. V.	Private	A	wounded
Lowe, W. E.	Private	A	wounded
Luchesi, David H.	Private	A	captured
Magill, Thomas F.	Private	B	wounded
Maguire, Charles E.	Cpl.	A	wounded
Marney, John	Private	A	wounded
Martin, John N.	Private	E	wounded
McCann, William V.	Private	C	wounded
McCormick, Henry A.	Private	A	killed
McGee, Daniel	Private	E	wounded
McGena, John	Private	C	wounded
McIntyre, George W.	Private	A	killed
McWilliams, James	Private	C	killed
Messick, Ross	Private	G	captured
Mills, Nicholas J.	1st Sgt.	F	wounded
Milstead, Joseph H.	Private	B	wounded
Moore, P. M.	Sgt.	E	wounded
Moore, Warren F.	Private	B	killed
Moran, William P.	Private	E	wounded
Morrison, Wilbur	Private	A	killed
Mulliken, Walter	Private	C	captured
Murray, William H.	Captain	A	killed
Nash, James	Private	C	wounded
Nicholai, Herman	Private	A	killed
Nichols, William L.	Private	C	wounded
O'Brien, James H.	Private	D	wounded
O'Byrn, John T.	Private	C	killed
Owings, Joshua	Cpl.	D	wounded
Payne, Benjamin	Private	C	killed
Peregoy, James A.	Private	A	captured
Pindell, Philip	Private	A	wounded
Polk, Samuel	Private	F	wounded
Probest, George	Sgt.	C	wounded
Radecke, Herman H.	Private	E	wounded

Reddie, James	Cpl.	E	wounded
Robbins, William	Private	G	wounded
Roberts, Frank	Private	E	wounded
Sanderson, Frank H.	Private	A	wounded
Schultz, Justus	Private	C	captured
Septer, John H.	Private	D	wounded
Shipley, William A.	Private	C	wounded
Simms, Thomas	Cpl.	B	wounded
Simms, William H.	Private	B	wounded
Skinner, William H.	Private	C	wounded
Smith, H. Tillard	Private	A	captured
Sollers, A. J.	Private	A	wounded
Starlings, George C.	Private	A	killed
Steele, Charles H.	Private	A	wounded
Steele, Frank K.	Private	C	wounded
Stewart, Thomas R.	Captain	G	wounded
Storm, Francis E.	Private	C	captured
Sullivan, John	Private	E	wounded
Taylor, Henry G.	Private	F	killed
Thelin, William T.	Private	A	wounded
Thomas, George	1st Lt.	A	wounded
Thomas, James W.	Sgt.	A	wounded
Thompson, John W.	Private	F	wounded
Tingle, D. B. P.	Private	G	wounded
Tolson, Thomas H.	2nd Lt.	C	wounded
Trail, Charles M.	Private	A	wounded
Trippe, Andrew C.	Private	A	wounded
Turner, Henry	Private	B	wounded
Turner, William L.	Private	B	wounded
Twilly, Benjamin F.	Private	G	wounded
Vickers, W. A.	Private	G	wounded
Wagner, Joseph S.	Sgt.	F	wounded
Wagner, R.	Private	F	wounded
Watts, William	Private	D	wounded
Weaver, L. H.	Private	G	captured
Webb, Emmett M.	Cpl.	D	wounded
Webster, James R.	Private	B	wounded
Welch, Edward A.	Cpl.	C	captured
Wheatley, William F.	Cpl.	B	wounded
White, John G.	Private	C	wounded
Wilkinson, William A.	Private	E	wounded
Williams, John P.	Private	A	wounded
Wills, James A.	Private	B	wounded
Wills, John W.	Private	B	wounded
Wilson, James H.	2nd Lt.	B	wounded
Windolph, John H.	Private	A	killed
Woolford, J. L.	Private	G	wounded
Wrightson, William C.	2nd Lt.	G	killed
Zollinger, Jacob E.	Private	A	wounded

Appendix B

Official List of Casualties

Taken from the Gettysburg Monument Report, published June 17, 1891

Third Maryland Infantry

Name	Rank	Co.	Remarks
Brown, J.	Private	F	wounded
Cocklin, Thomas	Private	E	wounded
Cummings, H.	Private	F	wounded
Fenton, Harry	Captain	G	killed
Hart, Matthew	Private	D	wounded
Miller, Peter	Private	I	wounded
Porter, Joshua	Private	K	wounded
Stevenson, John M.	Surgeon	Staff	wounded

First Regiment Eastern Shore Infantry

Adams, William	Cpl.	I	wounded
Andrews, Francis E.	Private	B	wounded
Arnold, Samuel J.	Private	C	killed
Carter, William	Private	C	wounded
Champlain, William R.	Private	H	wounded
Eaton, William H.	Private	E	killed
Giles, Robert	Private	H	wounded
Gossage, James H.	Cpl.	H	wounded
Hayman, Josephus H.	Cpl.	B	wounded
Hill, William	Private	C	wounded
Hull, William	Private	H	wounded
Jester, Charles H.	Private	H	wounded
Jones, William P.	Private	B	killed
Long, Henry C.	Private	K	wounded
Nickum, Samuel	Private	I	wounded
Perry, William E.	Private	E	wounded
Price, James E.	Private	H	wounded
Price, William H.	Private	H	wounded
Pritchett, Edward	Private	B	killed
Satterfield, Andrew	Private	H	wounded
Scott, James H.	Private	H	wounded
Sterling, Southey	Private	K	killed
Townsend, Alfred	Private	E	missing
Townsend, Joshua	Private	E	missing
Wolford, Joseph	Private	C	wounded

First Regiment Potomac Home Brigade

Abbott, Edward G.	Sgt.	I	wounded
Barger, Columber	Private	D	wounded
Barger, George	Private	H	killed
Bast, George M. D.	Private	I	wounded
Battee, Samuel	Sgt.	C	wounded
Baxter, Francis	Private	D	wounded
Baylis, Joseph	Private	I	killed
Beck, John J.	Cpl.	H	wounded
Bellis, Roger	Sgt.	D	wounded
Bender, George	Private	H	wounded
Besore, Oscar	Private	E	wounded
Billingsley, William T.	Cpl.	G	wounded
Booth, William H.	Private	D	wounded
Bowers, William	Private	H	wounded
Boyer, Peter	Private	E	wounded
Brace, John H.	Private	K	killed
Breighner, Samuel	Cpl.	G	wounded
Burk, William H.	Private	I	wounded
Caldwell, William	Private	A	wounded
Carnes, David L.	Private	I	killed
Caswell, Andrew	Private	H	wounded
Conner, John	Private	F	killed
Cunningham, James	Private	H	wounded
Dunlap, James	Private	I	missing
Dusing, Daniel D.	Private	E	wounded
Dye, John W.	Private	H	wounded
Eader, Charles E.	1st Lt.	I	killed
Easton, Elisha	Private	E	wounded
Farling, John J.	Private	A	killed
Fenory, Philip	Private	E	wounded
Fleagle, Uriah	Private	G	killed
Florey, Barney	Private	E	wounded
Ford, Stephen	Private	D	killed
French, Peter	Private	E	killed
Frizzle, Silas	Private	G	killed
Gormley, Matthew	Cpl.	K	wounded
Groff, Joseph	Captain	B	wounded
Hardesty, Frank H.	1st Lt.	G	wounded
Hardinger, Reuben	Cpl.	F	wounded
Harper, Lloyd M.	Cpl.	D	wounded
Hartman, Hiram H.	Private	F	killed
Hesson, Alpheus	Cpl.	B	killed
Hewitt, Daniel	Private	A	wounded
Hughes, Joseph L.	Private	F	wounded

Humes, Thomas J.	Sgt. Major	Staff	wounded
Inglebright, Michael	Private	F	wounded
Ingram, John	Private	A	wounded
Jackson, John W.	Sgt.	C	wounded
Jackson, Joseph A.	Private	A	wounded
Jamison, Robert	Private	C	wounded
Kelsey, Franklin	Private	A	wounded
Knepper, William D.	Private	F	wounded
Krebs, Daniel	Private	D	wounded
Krebs, David	Private	G	killed
Kuhn, Leander H.	Cpl.	D	wounded
Leidenstricker, Wm. H.	Sgt.	E	wounded
Lisle, John	Private	C	wounded
Lorentz, Lloyd M.	Private	D	wounded
Lowe, Caleb B.	Sgt.	G	wounded
Lowry, George G.	Private	K	killed
Marks, Benjamin	Cpl.	E	wounded
Marlow, Samuel	Private	E	wounded
Matthews, Sylvester	Private	G	wounded
Miller, Henry	Private	C	killed
Miller, Peter L.	Private	G	killed
Miller, Peter	Private	G	wounded
Miller, William	Private	F	wounded
Moffatt, William P.	Private	B	wounded
Must, George	Private	F	killed
Nuse, Hezekiah	Private	A	wounded
Picketts, Andrew	Private	B	wounded
Pierce, Richard	Sgt.	G	wounded
Proctor, William H.	Sgt.	E	wounded
Ray, Samuel	Private	D	wounded
Rhinehart, Charles	Private	B	wounded
Rippin, John J.	Private	D	wounded
Rohrer, William H.	Cpl.	I	wounded
Roulett, John	Private	A	wounded
Ryan, Michael	Cpl.	E	wounded
Sherbert, Daniel	Private	K	killed
Shew, Jacob	Private	G	wounded
Shriner, Lewis E.	Sgt.	D	wounded
Smith, Charles E.	Cpl.	C	wounded
Smith, James T.	1st Lt.	C	killed
Sosey, John M.	Private	F	wounded
Stall, Leopold	Sgt.	C	wounded
Stern, William H.	Cpl.	E	wounded
Stockman, John W.	Private	B	wounded
Strong, George	Private	C	wounded

Strong, William	Private	C	wounded
Thompson, George	Private	E	wounded
Thompson, William	Private	K	wounded
Turner, Edward	Private	C	wounded
Vance, Thomas	Private	C	killed
Wachter, Elijah R.	Private	I	wounded
Wain, George H.	2nd Lt.	C	wounded
Warner, Frederick G.	Private	F	wounded
Warner, Philip	Sgt.	F	killed
Wetherall, James P.	Cpl.	G	wounded
Wilhide, Daniel	Private	D	wounded
Willman, John L.	1st Lt.	D	killed
Wood, Robert	Cpl.	A	wounded
Yingling, William H.	Private	B	wounded

Appendix C

Roster of Maryland Soldiers in National Cemetery

SECTION A

No. of grave	Name	Co.	Regiment
1	Southey Stirling	K	1st Regiment, Md. V.
2	Unknown		
3	Wm. P. Jones	B	1st E. Shore Md. V.
4	Edward Pritchard	B	1st Regiment, Md. V.
5	Unknown		
6	Unknown		
7	Unknown		
8	H. Miller	C	1st Regiment, P.H.B.

SECTION B

No. of grave	Name	Co.	Regiment
1	Wm. E. Eaton	H	1st E. Shore Md. V.
2	G. H. Barger	H	1st Regiment, Md. V.
3	A. Saterfield	I	1st E. Shore Md. V.
4	Joseph Bailey	B	1st Regiment, Md. V.
5	Teter French	B	1st Regiment, P.H.B.
6	Unknown		
7	Stephen Ford	D	1st Regiment, Md. V.

SECTION C

No. of grave	Name	Co.	Regiment
1	G. W. Lowry	K	1st Regiment, P.H.B.
2	John Conner	F	1st Regiment, P.H.B.
3	David Krebe	G	1st Regiment, P.H.B.
4	M. F. Knott	F	1st Batallion CSA
5	Frank Baxter	D	1st Regiment, Md. V.
6	John W. Stockman		1st Brigade

SECTION D

No. of grave	Name	Co.	Regiment
1	Unknown, (killed at Hanover, Pa.)		

TOTAL, 22.

Appendix D

Marylanders Attending 75th Reunion in 1938

Army	Name	Address
US	Bramble, Goodman W.	111 Muse St., Cambridge
US	Cowgill, Stephen P.	Glenn Dale
CS	Dance, E. Scott	W. Chesapeake Ave., Towson
US	Daniels, Charles H.	1313 Linden Ave., Baltimore
US	Davis, Thomas	5009 Roland Ave., Baltimore
US	Fassett, Isaiah	Branch St., Berlin
US	Garlick, Joseph	R.1, Box 165, Cumberland
US	Hyland, Lambert	103 Pond St., Salisbury
US	Hynson, Sr., Joseph	Rock Hall
US	Jackson, Henry	Aikin
US	Jones, Spencer	Federalsburg
US	Leech, George T.	3725 Reistertown Rd., Baltimore
US	Leighty, George	Hancock
US	Liddell, John H.	3100 Oakford Ave., Baltimore
US	Martin, Bernard Banks	1612 E. Monument St., Baltimore
US	Medley, Richard	St. Inigoes
US	Mullinix, Francis Lincoln	61 S. Church St., Westminster
US	Pitts, Frederick	149 W. Henrietta St., Baltimore
US	See, Dallas M.	Queen Anne
US	Sines, John	R. 1, Oakland
US	Weaver, George W.	157 W. 37th St., Baltimore
US	Young, John N.	3304 Gwynns Falls Parkway, Baltimore

Appendix E

Citizens for a Maryland Monument in Gettysburg

Honorary Chairman
The Honorable
William Donald Schaefer
Governor of Maryland

Chairman
Mr. James A. Holechek

Board of Trustees
Mr. Tommy D'Alesandro, III
Ms. Jean H. Baker
Mr. Hal Donafrio
Mr. Harlow Fullwood, Jr.
Mr. Edwin F. Hale
Mr. David R. Hall
Mr. Jeffery C. Herwig
Hon. Martha S. Klima
Mr. Ronald E. Knowles
Mr. Reuben Kramer
Mr. Fred Lazarus, IV
Mr. J. Gary Lee
Hon. O. James Lighthizer
Mr. Thomas H. Sherlock
Col. Ernest M. Snyder, USA Ret.
Mr. Walter Sondheim, Jr.
Mr. Daniel Carroll Toomey
Mr. Edwin A. Warfield, IV
Mr. Courtney B. Wilson

Implementation Committee
Mr. Richards R. Badmington
Mr. Stephen R. Bockmiller
Mr. J. Steven Fayer
Mr. David R. Hall
Mr. Dale Hilliard
Mr. Ronald E. Knowles
Mr. J. Gary Lee
Mr. Thomas H. Sherlock
Mr. Daniel Carroll Toomey

INDEX

Alexander, E.P., 35
Armistead, Lewis A., 36
Andrews, Richard S., 1, 16, 18, 19
Andrews Battalion, 17
Archer, James J., 4
Army of Northern Virginia, 1, 4, 30
  Brigades
    Davis', 3
    Gordon's, 46
    Nicholl's, 19, 20
    Smith's, 28
    Stewart's, 1, 5, 6, 19, 20, 23
    Stonewall, 1, 7, 20, 23, 28
  Calvary, Stuart's, 3, 7, 30
  Divisions
    Early's, 2, 4, 20
    Johnson's, 1, 16, 19, 20, 22
    Pender's, 38
    Pickett's, 35, 36, 38
    Rodes', 4
Army of the Potomac, 11, 13
  Corps
    First, 4, 16
    Second, 1, 44
    Third, 14
    Sixth, 41
    Eighth, 13
    Eleventh, 4, 16, 21
    Twelfth, 9, 14-16, 20, 22, 28
Artillery
  Fourth Volunteer Brigade, 11

Baltimore City, 13, 16, 44, 45, 75
Baltimore Pike, 8, 11, 16, 27
Benner's Hill, 15, 16, 18, 19
Biesecker, F. W., 46
Bigelow's Battery, 9
Bison, James, 43
Berry, John S., 49
Bond, Frank, 5, 6
Breathed, James, 31, 32
Brinkerhoff's Ridge, 7, 8, 20
Brown, Lt. A, 6
Brown, Ridgely, 5, 6
Brown, Steuart, 50, 54
Brown, William D., 17, 18, 44
Buford, John 3, 4
Burlando, Father F., 41, 42

Cambridge, MD, 13
Carroll, Samuel S., 21, 23
Cashtown, PA, 3, 47
Cemetery Hill, 5, 16, 17, 20, 31, 45
Cemetery Ridge, 5, 9, 23
Charles County Mounted Volunteers, 16
Chew, Walter S., 18
Comegys, William, 27, 54
Cook, Addison, 16
Cook, Jacob, 18
Cook, Roger E., 26
Cooksville, MD, 3
Cress' Ridge, 32, 33
Culhane, Father W. F., 76
Culp, Wesley, 28
Culp's Hill, 5, 6, 9, 10, 14, 15, 19, 20, 23,
    27, 28, 32, 45, 49, 50
Curtain, Andrew 46, 49
Custer, George A., 33, 36

Dance, E. Scott, 75

DeFord, B., 49
Deems, James M., 34, 35
Dement, William F., 19
Dorsey, G. W., 30, 31
Douglas, Henry K., 1, 28, 29, 44
Duvall, Robert E., 3

Earl, George H., 75
Ellicott Mills, MD, 13, 46
Elzey, Arnold, 7
Emmitsburg, MD, 41, 75
Evergreen Cemetery, 16, 48
Ewell, James S., 1, 6

Fenton, Henry, 10
Fitzhugh, Robert H., 11
Fort, Allen T., 47
Ft. McHenry, 36
Frederick, MD, 3

Gardner, Alexander, 43
General Hospital, 44
Gettysburg Battlefield Memorial
    Association, 49-52, 58
Gibraltar Brigade, 21
Gibson, William, 71
Gilmor, Harry, 5

Goldsborough, William W., 7, 15, 20, 23-25, 28
Goodwin, C. Ridgley, 54
Gore, Henry, 45
Gordon, John B., 31
Graham, Dr. G. R., 71
G. A. R., 50, 53, 54, 71, 75
Green Mount Cemetery, 19, 44
Gregg, David, 8, 33
Griffin, William H., 33

Hagerstown, MD, 6, 18, 75
Hale, Charles A., 6, 18
Hanover Road, 8, 15, 33
Hartman, Hiram H., 46
Harrison, James, 3
Hatton, Samuel, 16
Heth, Henry, 3
Herbert, James R., 7, 20, 22, 28
Hicks, Thomas H., 11
Holliday, Henry, 48
Hollyday, Lamar, 50
Hobbs, N.C., 31
Hunt, Henry, 36

Jackson, E. E., 54, 58, 59
Johnson, Bradley T., 2, 7, 15
Johnson, Edward, 1

Kane, Thomas L., 28
Keener, Charles H., 43
Knott, Minion F., 46
Kramer, Samuel, 54
Krauth, John M., 51, 58
Krebs, David, 46

Laird, J. Winder, 28
Lang, Theodore F., 54, 58
Latchford's Drum Corps, 50
Latimer, Joseph W., 15, 18
Latrobe, Osmond, 36
Little Round Top, 5, 6, 15
Lockwood, Henry H., 8, 9, 54
Lockwood's Brigade, 9, 13, 14
Long, Littleton, 13
Love, William H., 69

McClellan Hotel, 42
McConaughy, David, 45, 49
McConnellsburg, PA, 5
McCurdy, Robert, 38
McIntosh's Brigade, 3, 8

McKim, Randolph, 1, 20, 21, 28, 51
McGilver, Freeman, 9
McGowan, Thomas, 46
McPherson's Ridge, 3
Manning, A. L., 14
Maryland National Guard, 6, 30, 50, 51, 54, 58
Maryland Units CSA
  Artillery
    1st, 15, 19
    2nd, 31
    4th, 15, 17, 18, 19
  Cavalry
    1st Battalion, 5, 31, 75
  Infantry
    1st Regiment, 19
    1st (2nd) Battalion, 1, 6, 7, 14, 15, 20, 24, 25, 27, 46, 48-51
Maryland Units USA
  Artillery
    Alexander's, 31
    Ribgy's, 11, 23, 54, 67
  Cavalry
    1st Regiment, 8, 20, 32, 35, 65
    Co. A Purnell Legion, 2, 8, 13, 20, 33, 69-71
  Infantry
    1st Potomac Home Brigade, 8, 9, 25, 26, 46, 61
    1st Eastern Shore, 9, 11, 13, 14, 25-27, 54, 58
    2nd Eastern Shore, 13
    3rd Regiment, 9, 10, 25, 58, 63
Massachusetts Units
  Infantry
    9th, 8
    20th, 43
Maulsby, William P., 9, 25
Mississippi Units
  Infantry
    21st, 9
Monocacy Bridge, MD, 9, 13
Moore, P.M., 27
Muhlenberg's Brigade, 22
Mullikin, James, 58
Muller, Louis, 43
Murray Association, 50
Murray, Alex, 25
Murray, Elizabeth, 44
Murray, William, 23-25, 28, 44

New Jersey Units
  Artillery
    1st, 33
  Calvary
    1st, 8
New York Units
  Infantry
    150th, 9, 27
Nolen, Frank, 54
North Carolina Units
  Infantry
    1st, 20
    3rd, 20
Parker, Thaddeus, 18
Parker, William J., 13
Parsley, W.M., 6, 20
Patapsco Guards, 46, 47
Pendleton, Sandy, 6
Pennsylvania Units
  Artillery
    Cooper's, 16
    Rank's, 3, 8, 13, 16
  Cavalry
    3rd, 32, 33
  Infantry
    3rd, 8
    29th, 25
    147th, 25
Probst, George, 50
Poplar Springs, MD, 13
Purnell, William H., 2
Powers Hill, 11, 81
Raine, C. T., 15, 18
Rayner, Isidor, 74
Regular Army, 4, 17, 21, 37
Reunion, 50th, 71, 73, 74
Reunion, 75th, 74-76
Rickett's Battery, 21
Ridgeville, MD, 14
Rigby, James H., 11
Roberts, Benjamin G., 18, 19
Rock Creek, 4, 20
Ross, Robert W., 27

St. Joseph Academy, 41
Sanitary Commission, 43
Seminary Hospital, 30
Seminary Ridge, 35, 41
Shepherd, Smith, 29
Sisters of Charity, 41, 42
Slocum, Henry W., 26
Smith, James T., 27

Soldiers National Cemetery, 46, 49
Spanglers Spring, 58
Steiner, John A., 26
Steuart, George H., 1, 7, 19, 28, 51
Stewart, James, 17
Stillson, J. B., 43
Stuart Horse Artillery, 31

Taneytown, PA, 14
Tener, John K., 74
Texas Units
  Infantry,
    5th, 4
Theological Seminary Hospital, 45
Thomas, George, 51
Trimble, Isaac R., 30, 37, 38
Turner, Roberty H., 14

United Confederate Veterans, 19, 75
U.S. Christian Commission, 43, 44

Van Bebber, Thomas E., 45
Vernon, George W., 54
Virginia Units
  Artillery
    Lee, 15
    Rockbridge, 15, 17
  Cavalry
    1st Regiment, 1, 2, 4
    35th Battalion, 1, 2, 4
  Infantry
    2nd, 8, 28
    9th, 36
    10th, 7, 23
    37th, 7

Wainwright, Charles S., 16
Wallace, James, 11, 27, 54
Walton, S. T., 7
Warren, E. T. H., 7
Weeks, Hezekiah, 46, 47
Wells, David, 46
Westminster, MD, 3, 14, 43
White, Elijah V., 1
White, Luther, 43
Willard, James, 9
Willeford, Richard H., 45
Williams, A. S., 9, 22
Wood, H. C., 7
Wrightsville, PA, 2, 46

Zollinger, W., 50